The Untold Truth Revealed

By Latoya Anderson

The Untold Truth Revealed

ISBN 978-1-304-60052-3

How lesbians prey on women's emotions and break down their mental state which causes their minds to become curious.

This book is dedicated to those individuals who
struggle with being themselves,
due to the fear of rejection.

Contents

Introduction

Chapter One: Emotional Breakdown

Chapter Two: Understanding Women and the Role to Play

Chapter Three: The Lesbo Charming System

Chapter Four: The Lesbo Pickup

Chapter Five: The Lesbo Conversion

Chapter Six: The Truth behind Lesbian Love

Chapter Seven: Sexing her Right

Chapter Eight: Eight Categories of the Lesbo System

Chapter Nine: My Lesbian Experience

Introduction

Homosexuality is defined as a romantic attraction, sexual attraction, or sexual activity between members of the same sex. Homosexuality is ultimately learned through a combination of molding factors and making personal choices. Societal attitudes toward same-sex relationships have varied over time and place, from expecting females to engage in long term relationships, acceptance, and casual integration. Society attitude towards homosexuals are rapidly changing to reflect greater acceptance from all nationalities. The GALLUP has proven that Americans acceptance of lesbians as equal members of society has increased steadily in the past decade to the point that more than half agree that being a lesbian is morally acceptable, lesbian's relations should be legal, and lesbians should be given equal opportunity to get married. Lesbians who love each other should be granted rights to openly celebrate their union or have a ceremony and have access to all marriage benefits as heterosexual couples. Women admire relationships to an extinct in such ways that the smallest mistake that her boyfriend/husband makes she is almost ready to immediately cease the relationship. Women are problem solvers and do not like to prolong a failing relationship that seem it will never heal. Women want a man to be someone they can rely on, depend on, and confide in along with making her feel happy, secure, and loved. However, when insensitive remarks, bitterness, and boring sex pile up in a long term relationship; the woman simply says enough is enough and begins to think about other options. Most women feel that men do little or nothing to solve problems, and as a result, the woman is frustrated and is ready to move to the next level of life where she feels love & acceptance. More and more women are leaving heterosexual relationships because they become emotionally attached to women. Most of the time these women become attached to women without having any clue a relationship will evolve. Lesbians use different tactics to draw these women close, and often times lead them to leaving their male companions.

The Marriage Builder indicates the two main reasons why women are eager to leave their friendships/marriage for other women are: (1) He is never there when they need him most and (2) He doesn't show any interest in her or what she does. Women are more likely to engage in same sex encounters for emotional satisfaction and eternal happiness. Boise State University conducted a research revealing that half of the women population is attracted to other women. Women get involve with other women using body languages and gestures. A quick way to evaluate yourself to see if your skills are appropriate for a particular setting is to just do it. By that I am saying, when women capture someone they see at first sight; they are observing the female. Once the woman has been observed and a conclusion is made that a possible connection is there; the personality is evaluated. At this point, the aggressor assumes from the body language of the female that they can get the woman to interact in the homosexual lifestyle, so they compliment her on how beautiful she looks, how the click of their heels make them smile, and so on. The most important factor is the aggressor. The aggressor has to present themselves as likable and keep good eye contact with their potential candidate. Once a friendship has been established and it is barely distinguishable from relationship, a pathway is opened for intimacy and romantic feelings to develop creating an unbreakable bond.

Homosexuality is on the rise and more & more women are engaging in lesbianism.

The question the world is asking is why women are seeking relationships with each other. The Untold Truth Revealed will explain in explicit content the lifestyle of a true lesbian.

The Emotional Breakdown

Men think women are complex, when actually they are very simple creatures. Most men tend to believe women are inconsistent and don't know what type of guy they are interested in. In reality, women have a great sense of what they want in a companion. Guys have this myth that women go from wanting the bad boy to the gentleman, from the gentlemen to the bad boy, then out of nowhere other women. What men don't quite understand, most women are interested in the individual who is confident and one who is capable of drawing emotional attraction. Emotional attraction is where the emotional aspect of a person draws you to them; this makes the individual want to be with or around you more than normal. In other words, an inseparable bond is formed that leads to a firm relationship. When it comes to women and their relationship the first question a woman will ask is. Will my partner be there to provide security? The second question is will my partner be there when I need it most? Most women look for someone who will provide them with the love and affection they require. Most men don't quite understand how to provide their women with the love and affection they need. I remember sitting down having a conversation with a couple of guy friends that are married, and explaining to them women emotions, and the attention they need. Although I went on and on about women and their emotions, they didn't understand the point I was making to them. I remember one of my friends not understanding why his wife complains every month during her menstrual cycle. He stated, "She know she's going to have these problems every month; why does she complain every month about something she knows is going to happen?" What he and the other guys didn't understand, this is a time when most women want and need affection. Yes their stomach is cramping and I understand you guys are thinking take some Midol but from the psychological stand point the quality time spent cuddling and rubbing her stomach eases so much more pain then telling her to take some Midol. This is where lesbian succeed and make a difference in their relationships. They understand the attention needed during this time and knows the female hormones are at a very high level and high levels causes' women to become more emotional and needy. Unlike some men lesbians will go the extra mile during this time because they know this is a way to stimulate the woman mind and interest. By the way, I don't want you to feel as if lesbians are the only one's capable of fulfilling women emotional needs, because there are guys who do an excellent job. This helps society understand how women become vulnerable to other women, and how lesbians use emotional attraction to draw women in. I use the conversation I had with my guy friends because it shows the importance of emotional attraction and gives a better idea of what emotional attraction is. In the conversation, my guy friend didn't quite understand the importance of his wife telling him she was cramping every month. Now women you know this is an emotional time for you, it all boils down to you hurting and wanting some attention to feel better so you moan and cry out to your partner for comfort. What the guys didn't understand that women are naturally emotional creatures and whatever emotion they are feeling they react to it, and expect their companion to react as well. Instead the guys laughed, and stated she should take some Midol. My friend failed to realize he was neglecting his wife's feelings when all she wanted was some affection. Another example how emotional attraction works, when a woman sees a friend is upset or their emotion is disturbing, women tend to become upset and feel the emotion as well. On the other hand if a male see a friend upset, he may feel the emotion for a moment then tune out the emotion and find ways to solve the problem. This is what happened in my friend case he did not do as women and sympathize with the pain his wife feels during her menstrual cycle; instead he tuned out her emotions and told her to take some Midol. This is where lesbian understand the emotions that are felt and react to the situation. We understand emotional attraction has a firmer foundation for a solid relationship. So many times we hear men say women are too emotional, and women complain men are tuned out emotionally. This is the prime reason women become intimate with other women and one reason I was able to develop an intimate relationship with my friend wife for several years. I'm not bragging about sleeping with his wife, in fact I feel bad about it but I was there to fill that emotional void when she needed it most. During the course of this relationship she discovered there was an emotional connection she thought never existed, and started to evaluate her previous relationships with men and felt it was impossible to connect with men emotionally. She even began to ask herself if she was a lesbian. I'm not going to go into details about this relationship until later, but the important thing to remember is that emotional attraction is the most important factor when it comes to having a solid relationship with women. This means paying attention to women emotions and consoling them during the most difficult times even when it seems a bit strange.

Understanding Women and the Role Played by a True Lesbians

When it comes to attracting women lesbians are the best at it, although there are some lesbians who are shy and lack confidence. The true lesbians understand the woman mind frame and skillfully influence some heterosexual women into the lifestyle. Society is constantly asking why so many women are converting to the homosexual lifestyle. Hopefully, at the end of this book, many will have an idea of how lesbian relationships are developed and understand how they differ from the heterosexual couple. True lesbians understand the role they play and understand women are looking for an aggressor who possess great social and leadership skills. An aggressor from the relationship point of view is someone who exhibits confidence and is capable of controlling the relationship, but keeps the relationship balance. This is very important to remember because most women are looking for someone who knows how to balance the relationship and provide them with security. When I speak about security I'm referring to the state of feeling safe and loved from the confidence you display. Yes, as lesbians, we must show a great amount of confidence to attract the women we desire, which I will discuss in another chapter. Pay close attention to this section because it plays a major role in the question a lot of people are asking. Why are heterosexual women leaving their male companion for another woman? This will also be explained in another chapter. I know you may be asking yourself, are security and aggressor the same qualities a male bring into a relationship? Yes they are, but lesbians are a different type of aggressor and provide security in a different way. Again, your question will be answered later. The main focus here is to understand the role lesbians have to play in order to successfully attract women. We have already established what women are looking for, so the next question is how do lesbians go about sparking her interest, and how do we come off attractive to her? Here's how, first we have to become familiar with the role to play. There are two roles you play in a relationship; you are either the aggressive individual or the passive. Take a minute and think what role you play when it comes to your relationships. Before I continue I'm going to explain the aggressive and passive individual, just like heterosexual relationships there always has to be balance for a relationship to work. When I speak of balance in the relationship, you usually have an aggressive individual dating the passive individual, we all know opposites attract. A relationship is not balanced if you have two aggressive individuals dating or two passive individuals dating. Although society looks at women as the passive, submissive individual, there are aggressive women as well. If you are asking if women are more passive, how do lesbians have balance in their relationship? Let me refresh your memory. Homosexual relationships work like heterosexual relationships, so when two women get involved one still is the aggressor and the other is passive. There's always an aggressive individual and a passive individual. It's also important not to confuse the term with its meaning, look at it from a relationship point of view. The aggressor is the individual who's more outspoken, charismatic, and brings confidence while the passive individual is more of the reserved individual. Throughout this book we will look at the role played in a relationship from the aggressor standpoint, because these are the lesbians who have great success when it comes to pursing the woman they desire. No matter the sexual orientation, the role we play doesn't change the dynamics. When it comes to attracting women one of the most important keys to lesbians are social and leadership skills. It may sound a little foolish, but we know women are attracted to those who know how to entertain them and others. Now think about it, when you meet a woman you find interesting and decide to go out on that first date; the objective is always to impress her. In order to impress her you must socialize about things that draw her attention to even be considered for a second date. Having great social and leadership skills draws women's attraction to a degree where they will do anything to make sure you are well taken care of. As lesbians we understand our social skills have to be so great that we have to attract followers, when this happens we find women wanting to be around us day in and day out. This shows women you have the ability to lead the relationship and make them feel valuable and possibly happier than they have ever been. Here's an example of what I mean, I use to work at a local department store with a lot of women who were classified as heterosexuals. When I started working there I had the most difficult time working with these women because of my lifestyle. I laughed when they use to turn their nose up and gossip all day about me being gay. This one particular day I overheard their conversation about the problems they were having with their boyfriends in the break room, so I took it upon myself to pull aside the woman I found most attractive and submissive and gave her a little advice and told her to try it. A couple of weeks later she would come by my department and thank me for my advice and ask for more advice. Eventually we became close and her friends became curious why we were conversing. Once she explained everything to them they classified me as cool, we began hanging out and I ended up sleeping with two of the five women. See, what I did here was use one of them to get the others to follow and I used the conversation they were most interested in to become friends with all of them. They considered me as cool, but this is the leadership and social skills I used to get what I wanted. Once a woman notices your leadership skills and interaction with others you will draw her attention and just like a magnet she is drawn in. This seems easy, but it's a tough task to manage when you are the passive individual. Don't get me wrong, I'm not talking about the passive individual who know their role and stay within it, I'm speaking of the individuals who seek the aggressor role. I'm referring to the passive lesbian who wants to be the aggressor and pursue the women they desire. I'm talking about that lesbian who would have let the women in the department store talk about her although she had a crush on one of them. Most of these individuals are passive lesbians because they are afraid of rejection. In order to become successful and attract the women that's more desirable, you have to gain social and leadership skills. Most passive individual shy away from the women they desire, because they don't pose enough confidence, they are afraid to initiate a conversation, because they have never been the person that's center of attention. When I say center of attention I don't mean being loud and noticeable but being the likeable person that everyone loves to be around. How this is done, by simply becoming the aggressor. This doesn't mean you change your personality and become that person who finds yourself mistreating women or having that badass mentality. What I'm saying is never allow fear and your emotions to take control of you. I'm not saying you are not allowed to express your emotional side, because as women we are all a bit emotional. It simply means stop being afraid of rejection, when or if you are rejected move on, and don't allow yourself to feel unconfident and miserable. This is when women sense they have control and causes them to dislike the role you have taken. Remember women are attracted to someone who keeps them in their perspective role, and that role is submissive. If you are the aggressive individual you have a difficult task as well, and they are just as tough as the passive individual. Unlike the passive individual, the aggressor poses a great amount of confidence, usually is the likeable person, knows how to socialize with others and spark women interest. So the question is what task I'm talking about, because it seems the aggressive individual knows how to maintain their relationship. Once you get the woman you desire, the aggressor duties are keeping the woman in their perspective roles and maintain balance. This becomes complicated because sometimes the aggressor has to make solid decision their women won't agree with. Often time these big decisions cause confusion and the relationship becomes rocky. When this happens the aggressive individual must remember they are in control and to never give in and become the passive individual. The most important thing the aggressor must do is find a way to balance things out, when the relationship has become rocky. I've discovered when the aggressor makes big decisions that may affect the woman attitude; they must find ways to change the negative vibe into a positive one. This is where most of these individuals fail, the relationship goes from good to bad then bad to worst because the aggressor is not able to maintain their relationship and it seems one argument leads to another one. When the relationship heads in this direction and she seems fieriest, counter that by rewarding her. The reward does not have to be an expensive gift; the biggest gift to give women is affection. The gift is simple as caressing her from behind and telling her how much you appreciate her. I know you may be asking yourself why reward her after making a sound decision, will this mean I'm becoming passive. No it doesn't, it means you made a decision and that decision stands but her feelings are important as well. This is a tactic that keeps women in their perspective roles, and blows them off their feet. True lesbians use this tactic a lot to keep their women drawn to them. I'm not quite sure if men use this tactic because of their egos, but if you are, you know the success, and if you haven't I suggest you change your method. Negativity during the toughest times of a relationship causes women to experience different emotions that leaves them depressed and causes them to leave. Showing appreciation during the most difficult times makes women feel valuable. When they are exposed to this emotion your relationship becomes impossible to break and it will have them eating from the palm of your hand.

The Lesbo Charming System

Before you can have any woman eating from the palm of your hand, a relationship has to be established. Lesbians have the most difficult time getting with the women we desire because nine times out of ten they are classified as heterosexuals and haven't experienced the homosexual lifestyle. The one way we draw these women into the lifestyle is through the lesbian charming system. When it comes to charming women the most important factor is confidence. Many will say if that's the most important factor when it comes to a woman, that's a piece of cake. For some that maybe true, but what's misunderstood is having confidence is more than believing you are attractive because you are told on the regular, or wearing that expensive outfit with your nose in the air because no one else can afford it. Don't get me wrong those are great qualities that boost your confidence, but true confidence are displayed when one has the ability to charm others around them. That's the system lesbians use on those beautiful self assured women they never thought were attracted to women. Hell, they didn't know they were attracted to women until they became victims of the lesbian charming system. Before I continue let me clarify all lesbians do not display these characteristic, but this chapter will be a great asset to those who have trouble with approaching and charming women. In the lesbian charming system the first stage is the belief system. In this stage we believe we are able to attract any and every woman we find attractive. It may not be the case, but it's the belief that we have and that comes from understanding even if the situation doesn't turn out how we like, we are still in control of it. This means if we find success with women then we created that moment, and if we fail with women then we are responsible for that as well. We understand that women like persistence, if you are able to show you are likeable and trustworthy then your chances become greater. During the belief stage there's no room for second guessing yourself it makes you unattractive and pushes the woman away. That's why confidence is the most important factor when it comes to charming women. Believe it or not women know instantly when meeting an individual how far things would go. So this means there's no time for a lack of confidence and to express shyness.

When this happens, the belief system has not become apart of your psychological mind frame, which means you have to motivate yourself to the point you believe I control the situation, by building self esteem. I remember when I first went off to college and noticed one of my suitemates, she was gorgeous, and she had the most beautiful smile and amazing face I've ever seen. Several months passed and I noticed she had a boyfriend, which made me a little more intimidated. I lacked confidence and felt she was too attractive and wouldn't even consider having me as a friend, yet along a companion. I eventually became obsessed and unnoticeably following her around to her classes. As I reflect back, I remember feeling desperate and helpless because I didn't know how to approach this female. I hated the feeling so I decided to evaluate one of the lesbians around campus, and noticed the confidence she possessed, and the self esteem she had. I disliked her because she boasted about the women she slept with and how she could get any woman she wanted. Although I disliked this individual arrogance, I learned through my evaluation she was a confident individual who developed great social and leadership skills. She knew what to say, when to say it, and smiled to charm every woman she came in contact with. I decided to use her skills and become more open because I realized in order to charm women social and leadership skills was a key component. I used these skills for the first time on the suitemate I was attracted to but they didn't work the first couple of times. She ignored me like I didn't exist. I went back to the drawing board and realized I was faking confidence. I didn't believe I was in control of the situation when she gave me attitude I dropped my head, walked away, felt embarrassed, and said, "I never should have approached her." After reevaluating, I built my confidence, which mode my self esteem, became the likeable person everybody loved, then I approached my suitemate again and was successful this time around. Now you can see the importance of confidence when charming women, it's an important factor as well as raising your social value. When you gain these skills it makes the approach so much easier and helps during the interacting stage. When I approached my friend the final time; I realized I created a flow. Instead of approaching her with Hey, how are you, I walked to her with an enormous amount of confidence and told her you should get rid of that attitude, I'm not that bad of a person then walked off with a smile. As I walked off I watched her stand there watching me with a smile. At this point I realized I was able to create a flow by teasing her and making her smile. What I mean by teasing her is showing her I was a nice and genuine person that had a sense of humor. The next time we met she sparked a conversation that eventually led to us becoming best friends, then later companions. When interacting with women it's very important to create a flow that shows women you are genuine and have a great sense of humor. You can not charm women if you are stuck on yourself. When charming women, another key factor lesbians understand is the importance of making women feel they're beautiful. This is done by simple compliments, which makes her feel important and confident as well. Women pose this confidence and have this mentality when they step out they are the sexiest woman ever. Think about it, they may wear their finest handbag, outfit or pumps, get their nails done, wear that glamour's eye shadow, or get that banging hairstyle that makes them feel stunning. In fact a woman's weakness is her need to look good. So we as lesbians use these things to our advantage by observing and complimenting their beauty. When we compliment that individual we make it our business to make the woman feel appreciated. Fortunately, there's always something to compliment women on, but the key is observing it. Whatever you find to compliment the woman on, the objective is to always make her feel astonishing and to create a flow.

The Lesbo Pickup

Throughout this next chapter I will explain how lesbians use their charming skills to successfully pickup the women they desire. This is the stage where attraction begins. This is the point where lesbians scope out particular women they find attractive. During the first stage of attraction no conversation is initiated, most lesbians make themselves noticeable to the individual they are seeking, and usually try to leave some type of impression. This is usually done by exhibiting a likeable personality, being respectful to her, or saying a simple hello. Stop and think for a minute if you meet someone who doesn't like you nine times out of ten you probably won't be friends, but if you meet someone who likes you and finds your personality intriguing, more than likely you will develop a friendship. That's how all relationships are formed. The key is being a likeable person. After we observe the individual we find interesting, a subconscious evaluation is conducted on that person to determine where she falls in the eight lesbian categories. These eight categories will be explained in a later chapter. During the evaluation we decipher one of two things, if we feel the woman will potentially invest their time in us or if we will get rejected. Most lesbians feel that women are curious creatures anyway, so that makes the task a bit easier. Before we continue, remember these techniques are used by the open lesbians, but not all lesbians master these skills and become successors with women. Once we have formed an opinion and decide where the woman fall in the lesbian eight categories we determine how much success we will have by observing the tone she use during a conversation, her body language and facial expression when we are around. If the woman initially gives off a negative vibe, she either doesn't like the lifestyle, which we process as the last resort, or we haven't made that big of impression on her which is more likely the case. When we haven't succeeded in making ourselves likeable the process starts over again and a different approach is taken to impress her. The most important key to lesbian success with women is exhibiting the likeable characteristic; no relationship can evolve without the other person feeling you are likeable, and this is done by simply doing the things we do well, and that's charming women. This is where the importance of being able to charm women comes in to place, if you haven't mastered the

technique to charming women; then
the process of reevaluating yourself
and confidence comes into play. When
a woman has a positive attitude about
you and you've become likeable in her
eyesight, you probably have impressed
her, and she finds something attractive
about you. This doesn't mean she
wants a relationship, but she probably
sees some positive characteristics in
you that are the same qualities she has
on her dating list, which we all know
women have these dating list. This is
when lesbians realize they have
entered the friend zone and the
objective is to push ourselves out of
the friend zone while the attraction is
there. If we become successful and
enter the friend zone more than likely
we have shown the qualities of being
loyal, trustworthy, likeable, and
outgoing, and we know all of these
qualities can lead to intimacy. These

qualities are developed between the two through enriched, enjoyable conversations. When you've reached this point it's important to pay close attention to her reactions, because you don't want to get stuck in the friend zone. The objective is always to move from the friend zone to the lure stage. As lesbians we understand if we don't focus in on the signals she gives, it's a possibility we will lose the attraction she has for us, when the attraction is lost its hard to gain back. So it's important to gain her attraction and lure her in, once we have recognized we have gained her attraction. If you're wondering why it's important to keep her attraction and lure her in? It's because most heterosexual women don't want to put themselves out there like that and they aren't always open to tell us that they will engage in the activity. On the other hand they will do spontaneous things to get our attention; it's left to us to lure her in. When women reach this point, lesbians know they have gained the woman trust and it's a matter of time before things reach the intimacy stage. I mentioned earlier lesbian reads into women reactions by observing their body language, tone of voice, facial expression, eye contact, and how playful they are. Once we've become certain she's attracted to us, she will use one of these signals and expect us to react to it. This is where we as lesbian seize the moment and take full advantage and begin the luring process. This is done with charm and confidence. We all know women loves to be charmed and complimented, so we as lesbians compliment women on the simplest things that will acquire a positive reaction. Remember this all takes place during the friend zone; we always establish a friendship with these women before we pursue anything further. Once we've complimented her time after time and notice her doing things such as, dressing in a manner that will grab our attention, start asking us to do certain activities with her, she makes strong eye contact with us, or she becomes touchy. We use this to our advantage and push things to the intimacy stage. When we reach this stage the one thing we are aware of, we can't put ourselves in the position where we are chasing her or pressing the woman into this stage, we must make her comfortable, to the point it's her own will to engage in the activity. During this stage it's important to pay attention; you will observe her doing the craziest things to impress you. We understand forcing ourselves on her will not only prevent the intimacy stage from happening but ruin the friendships, so it's critical that we have observed her actions and certain there's an emotional connection before we make a move. This brings us to the final point which is breaking through. After we have noticed changes such as her batting her eyes, smiling when she comes around us, and her acknowledging she wants to be around us more, we began to break through those barriers that get us to the intimate stage. These barriers are broken in many different ways, which will be explained in a little bit but they are used from a psychological standpoint. I mentioned in the previous chapters that women are emotional creatures and they react on emotions. Well, lesbians understand if we are capable of being that likeable, attractive, outgoing individual in her eyesight, then we are definitely capable of weaken her mind and seducing her into the activity. When we are confident we have built emotional comfort and emotional attraction we break through the intimate stage with sexual playfulness. The main goal of sexual playfulness is either to develop an intimate relationship or to establish a relationship as companions. When using sexual playfulness it's very important to never take things too serious and to never be too aggressive, patience is the key. Being serious and over aggressive can cause us to lose everything we have built. We lose our friendship and the possibility of a relationship ends. Although she may seem comfortable and show signs of interest, most of these women (speaking of the heterosexual) are still nervous and not sure if they want to engage in the act. Sexual playfulness begins in the friend stage and is used more frequently when we reach the intimate stage until we get what we desire. So what is sexual playfulness and how is it used? Sexual playfulness is nothing more than a friendly act that builds sexual tension, and is used to get women mentally prepared to engage intimately with the same sex, this is done by simply touching her. The key is to understand how far to go in each stage, too much touching in the friend zone can cause problems and result in a loss of friendship. I stated earlier that it is important not to be over aggressive and serious, this will only cause the woman to end the friendship. Once she ends the friendship, it becomes impossible to gain back. When I reach the friend zone I use confidence and my charming ways to become successful at sexual playfulness. For instance, when I become friends with a woman, I become very observant, if I notice her nails are done I immediately use sexual playfulness by asking her to show me her nails. When she hold up her hand, I would grab and hold her hand about five to six seconds while I stroke one of her finger from the knuckle to the tip of the nail with my thumb, then I look her directly in the eye and compliment her on how beautiful her nails are. This is a friendly touch that only takes about five to six seconds. The objective of the touch in the friend zone is to show your interest by complimenting her, but the most important thing is recognizing her reaction. Usually when I stroke her finger and look in her eyes, I get the biggest smile ever, this technique weakens her mind and most importantly it shows her she's appreciated and makes her feel astounding when she receive compliments. During the friend zone the touches are limited to the fingers, hands, and arms. The touch has to be sensual and creative in both the friend and the lure stage. In the lure stage she usually becomes friendlier than in the friend stage, and the objective is to push her out of the friend zone with sexual playfulness. During the lure stage the touches become longer and we are able to explore more areas such as the back of the neck, shoulders, lower back, waist, hip and butt. Earlier I explained the difference between each stage, in the lure stage I stated that it's important to observe her playfulness, eye contact and, body language. Women give off different signals that let us know she's possibly ready for the intimate stage. When in the lure stage touches can last anywhere from six to twenty seconds, and can be repeated. The objective is to make her comfortable first and then get her wondering what sex is like with the same sex. During this stage the touches are sensual and good judgment is required to know whether to push things forward or to back off and repeat the friend zone steps. This is where it's very important we pay close attention to her reactions, because messing up in this stage will surely ruin our chances forever. When I notice I have reached the lure stage I use my creative mind to push things into the intimate stage. Here's an example, after I've become friends with a woman and notice she's asking for more time to spend together, this is usually my cue to push things into the lure stage. Nine times out of ten if she's asking to spend more time, this means she's comfortable and probably going to do something to get my attention. It never fails, that's how women operate. If they are interested they are going to try to catch your eyes, but it's important for us to notice, and then lure them in. Anyway, when we began spending more time, I might notice the tight pants she wears when she comes around, and I will immediately use sexual playfulness to gain control. The first thing I would do in a playful manner is tell her your pants hugging those hips aren't they. This makes her aware that I notice the tight pants she's wearing and also compliment her at the same time. When she smiles I know it's ok to make a move, so I would stand behind her and quickly insert one of my fingers in the back of her pants and slightly pull her towards me. If she doesn't order me to stop, I repeat the same thing about three to four times until I have pulled her close to me. If she continuously smile and never give me a command to stop, I know I have successfully lured her in. When it's obvious we have lured her in we reach the final stage which is the intimacy stage. During the intimacy stage it's important to be sure that an emotional connection has been formed. Without an emotional connection the possibility of a relationship becomes impossible. In the example I gave in the lure stage, I knew I built that emotional connection when I put my finger in her pants, pulled her close to me and she smiled. At that moment I knew it was ok to make a sexual pass at her. During the intimate stage this is done by testing her with a kiss on the cheek, close to her lips. If the emotional connection is there and sexual playfulness was used correctly during the intimacy stage, some form of relationship will develop. When most of these heterosexual women have their first romantic encounter they become confused about the situation and often times step back. The key is to give her a little time to process the ordeal, but it's important to comfort her because she is probably going to experience a lot of emotions. Pushing things back to the friend zone is the key here, once she deals with the situation and gets a grip on everything a romantic relationship will probably evolve if the sex is great, and then the lesbian conversion begins.

The Lesbo Conversion

More and more heterosexual women are converting to the homosexual lifestyle today and the question many are asking is why? Some believe these women were physically, sexually and/or emotionally abused so they turn to another woman for comfort. Although that is true in many cases, there are also other factors that cause women to convert to the homosexual lifestyle. As I've mentioned throughout this book women are emotional creatures and they act off their emotions. Steve Harvey quoted, "Our love isn't your love" in his book, Think like a Man Act like a Lady, and I agree with him. I've seen so many married women miss the emotional connection with their husbands, because their husbands feel they have to be the bread winner, the provider, they spend more time making sure the family is financially stable, and forget his wife needs emotional support. In this time and era things have changed for women. More and more women are becoming successful in the corporate world and the role as a stay at home mom is decreasing. I understand the male perception of stability, but all relationships have to have balance, and the need of both partners has to be met. I've had great success with heterosexual women because I was able to recognize the weakness in their relationships. Most of them complained about the quality time they weren't getting from their partner. Some even felt they had more responsibilities in their relationship. A lot of times these women express themselves to their lady friend and find comfort in them. In most cases if that lady friend happens to be a lesbian this is where the conversion begins. When we are able to recognize a woman having problems with their male companion; we automatically assume that relationship has no balance, and if we find her interesting we make it our business to fill that void. We eventually make our way in the friend zone and develop an emotional connection. When an emotional connection is formed; the woman escapes from the problems that exist in her relationship, and began focusing on the attention her lady friend is giving her. This happens when the woman realizes the connection she longs for becomes present in another woman. When the quality time she longs for from her male companion gets filled from another woman things become fun and exciting for her. When I speak of quality time I'm not using this in reference to taking her out to dinner, or sitting watching movies with her. I'm using this in regards to being able to communicate more openly. Here's the thing when women get together nine times out of ten there's a lot to be discussed amongst them. Most men think it's just gossip, when actually women carry a lot of emotions and just want to vent about those emotions. You're probably wondering what this has to do with the reason straight women leave men for lesbian. The reason is because as lesbians and as women we have the ability to naturally feel her emotions and communicate at the same time, unlike men. When women realize someone is there to fill the emotional void, a comfort level is built. When this comfort is built a deeper bond is formed and she began to experience feelings she never felt with her male companion. This is when she starts to question herself and feel as if men can't fill that emotional void. One thing about the transition women become attached to the emotional connection rather than the gender. Meaning her subconscious mind forget about the woman being a woman. It's the charisma, openness, sense of humor, and the trustworthiness lesbians show that attracts these women. When the gender becomes obsolete and the emotional connection takes over, the woman usually makes the decision to leave her male companion.

Earlier I stated that some women I have dated felt there was too much responsibility in their relationship. Most of these women were overwhelmed at the fact that their male companion expected them to tackle too much of the household activities. Well, you are probably thinking that's a woman's duty, and I agree with you, but those duties can get stressful. When it comes to the homosexual lifestyle the overwhelming burden of household duties becomes the responsibility of both partners. When a lesbian interact with a straight woman and find ways to help her with some of those responsibilities; the woman becomes aware of the 50/50 relationship, and she no longer feels all the responsibilities are on her. This makes things that much sweeter and lift that overwhelming burden off her shoulders and open the door to more excitement.

When heterosexual women engage in a friendship with homosexual women their minds become more open through communication. The main point here is that lesbians use emotional connection to get close to the women they are pursing. As I've explained in previous chapters if we are capable of developing a friendship and these women perceive us as likable, convincing them to convert to the homosexual lifestyle becomes a piece of cake.

The Truth behind Lesbian Love Making

This is the section where I spice things up and introduce the pleasures women encounter with other women, and explore that question both men and women or asking all around the world. What can a woman do with another woman besides engage in oral sex or grind one another? Well I'm going to tell you that is a myth. It's also a myth women become intimate with other women because men don't satisfy them sexually. Stop and think for a minute, if you classify yourself as heterosexual. Did you consider being straight because a homosexual didn't satisfy you? I didn't think so; well it's the same for women who lives or partakes in the homosexual lifestyle. Women become involved with other women because they value the emotional side of a relationship. This is where most guys fail because they don't realize the importance of the emotional side of women. Women need more attention than guys realize and what tends to happen when their needs are not met they usually express their feelings and emotions to their female friends which open the door to an intimate relationship. When this connection is made between two women, a bond is formed and leads women to partake in the homosexual lifestyle, and that becomes a problem for some men. Especially when their woman leaves them for another female, this will be discussed in another chapter but I must explain the bitterness some men have when it comes to lesbians.

I've ran across several men who exhibit this negative attitude when it comes to dykes. This is the terminology they use when they call themselves degrading or belittling lesbians. I've sat with guys during these conversation and intruded in some conversations I was not apart of, to learn they are not degrading lesbians because they dislike them, but intimidation is the factor. Most of these guys will call this some bullshit, but remember earlier I said the most important characteristic to have with women is confidence, so when you're confident intimidation doesn't exist. This means if you are as confident as you say you are other relationships should not be a factor. What I find most intriguing, the same guys who boast about how they put it down and how they make their women cum in twenty minutes are the same guys posting negative messages on social media websites about lesbians, giving strange looks to couples when they're out, and spend a lot of time chit chatting with their homies on this topic. I'm not only confronting guys, this goes for some of the women out there as well. If you are one of those who just don't understand the lesbian lifestyle, or if you are that person wondering what goes on behind closed doors, or that person always getting mad asking what can two women possibly get from sex? I'm about to open your eye as well as your mouth and expose the truth behind lesbian love.

While sex with most men is phallic-centered and revolves around intercourse, and that can be limiting and unsatisfying for some women, there can be a lack of emotional intimacy with men. There's a connection between women that some men never reach. How do I know? I've experienced the emotional realms after sex with women and because I've dated several women who have dated guys and those that were married. All these women have stated they have not experienced the emotional intimacy with their male companion. Do I consider myself a pro of all pro's? Yes! The next question you may ask is why, because I have worked extremely hard on building confidence and the confidence I have proclaimed has become factual. Meaning it's instilled in me, there's nothing fake about it. See there's no doubt in my mind every time

I'm sexually active with a woman I accomplish the goals I intend. You may think I'm arrogant or maybe over confident, but your thoughts alone will not change factual information. This book is not for me to prove the confidence I have when it comes to women, but it's to make you realize women love companions who are confident and knows how to satisfy them sexually.

When it comes to sex there are three stages to remember the, orgasmic mind, romance, and climax. The first and most important stage is orgasmic mind. This is the state of mind you put women in before sex, and keep them present during sex. The orgasmic stage leads you to the romance stage and determines the height of the climax. If you are capable of igniting her mental state, most likely you will produce the most incredible, intense orgasm she's ever experienced. On the other hand, if you fail to ignite her mental state more than likely you will not experience the full body orgasms women are capable of having. One thing to remember, the mind controls what her body produces; this means her body only produces if she's relaxed. This is when you become responsible for her relaxation. During sex women can be a little self conscious and allow so many things to block them from the orgasmic state. Women are emotional creatures and during sex different emotions are exposed. Often times they are not comfortable with their body parts, or wondering what their partner thinks about them. This is why the emotional intimacy between two women is greater than most men are capable of producing. See, most lesbians recognize and understand the different emotions going through women mind before sex, and they know the purpose is always to please the woman before self pleasure. On the other hand, most men aren't thinking about what type of emotions women are feeling when its time for sex.

They believe when its time to get it on, that means just that. Guys don't have to turn on the mental switch when it times for sex, but it's a totally different story with women. So, how do you get her in the orgasmic mind? Simply understanding her emotion, build relaxation, and maintaining relaxation. Understanding her emotions can be quite difficult for some, but you can identify those emotions through body language. If you observe her body language as relaxed, building relaxation becomes an easy task to maintain. The keys to successfully keeping her mind in a orgasmic state during sex is giving her soft plausible touches, soft gentle kisses while complimenting her, and making her feel sexy. Remember the objective is always to please the woman and to engage all her senses. Engaging her senses means complimenting her, stroking her body gently, while ordering her to relax her mind and get lost. All these different combinations should arouse her and brings all the attention to her pussy, but you should not over heat her in the first stage.

This brings us to the next stage which is romance; this stage consists of building anticipation until she reaches the highest point of climax. In laming terms this is when you begin to perform sexual acts. This stage requires an enormous amount of foreplay. So, what is foreplay? Foreplay is a set of emotional intimate acts between two people meant to create sexual arousal and desire. Unlike men, women are not mentally and physically ready to have sex. Foreplay stimulates the woman mind and leads to the most powerful orgasms women can reach. Because foreplay is missed during sexual encounter so often, emotional intimacy is never reached. Once again this is where lesbian succeed and understand the importance of foreplay. You can't tell a woman lets have sex and expect her to have a full body orgasm; it does not work that way. When I speak of foreplay I'm talking about making her feel so over heated when you penetrate her pussy her eyes roll in her head, and you can feel her moans within. There are different techniques when it comes to foreplay, but I suggest exploring every inch of her body from top to bottom. Lets go back a minute, I know you are probably trying to distinguish the difference between stroking her body in the orgasmic stage to exploring her body in the romance stage. Here's the difference in the orgasmic stage the woman should never be heated to the point of climax that exist in romance. To make this simple, in the orgasmic stage sexual acts is not allowed for example foreplay or penetration, during the romance stage penetration is initiated. Now that we have distinguished from orgasmic to romance, I will continue with how to initiate foreplay. When initiating foreplay a mood should always be created, I'm not saying candles and music have to spark the moment which is nice at times, but the female mind has to be relaxed. I'm reiterating this because its very important for the woman to stay in the orgasmic mindset otherwise she will not reach her highest peak in the climax stage. When you observe your woman in the orgasmic state, and you begin to be intimate remember to be gentle. Stroke and kiss her body with softness, explore her body from top to bottom by rubbing and nibbling her ear, neck, collarbone, breast, stomach, side, pelvic, inner thigh, vagina, and feet. Once you explored her spots and have an idea what's her favorite, which probably would be her inner thigh and vagina area since she's in the orgasmic state. Take time to massage that area while you kiss other area. The intensity from foreplay will eventually lead to the climax stage.

The climax stage is the stage in which women experience the most intense orgasms ever, these orgasms are called squirting, and full body orgasm. Women experience these orgasms through penetration, but not every woman experience these orgasms. It takes time and technique. So many women complain of never having a vaginal orgasm, and the reason nine times out of ten is because the orgasmic stage is skipped and most individuals are so excited about their pleasures, women get cut short before they are able to reach the climax. I've asked several women I've dated before being intimate with them. Have you ever had an orgasm so powerful you experienced some type of liquid shoot across the room? Most of all the women I've asked gave me a weird look and responded no. This amazes me because so many women are getting cut short of one of the most incredible feelings they will every experience during sex. I mention earlier the orgasmic mind leads to romance, and romance, leads to climax. This is true, but you're not capable of producing squirting and full body orgasms during the climax stage if you can't incorporate the orgasmic mind and romance stage. I'm not going into squirting and full body orgasms now, because you have to understand female anatomy in order to produce these orgasms. Later in the chapter I would explain the female body parts that trigger full body and squirting orgasms. For now I will give you an idea of what to expect. The climax stage is the most powerful stage of them all, when you reach this stage and able to produce you become a pro of all pro's. You gain this great amount of confidence and you start to challenge women because you feel you have this power that controls them. I say this because studies have shown over seventy percent of women never experienced a squirting and full body orgasm, that's a huge number. This means a lot of women are missing out. When a woman experience orgasms in the climax stage there's so many emotions she will display, some may cry, inquire about the things her body experience, go crazy and become attach a little more then you expect. I know you wondering what happens during this stage that causes women to become emotional. Unlike men women act on emotions, if something makes her feel good there's a reaction to that. When a woman reaches the highest point in the climax stage she produces liquids you probably never experience before. These liquids are called female ejaculation and often mistaking for urine. The liquid comes out the woman urethra, the hole in which the woman urinates from, not the hole where the woman is penetrated. It may seem like urine but its not it comes from the woman prostate glands. So yes women do ejaculate and is capable of producing multiple squirting orgasms. When this happen, women usually feel the urge to pee and hold back due to embarrassment, but if she relax and release, it will make the orgasm more intense. This type of orgasm develop from penetration and when the woman push the ejaculation out she gets to experience the other type of orgasm during the climax stage which is called the full body orgasms I like to keep the two separate because you are able to identify when a woman is doing both. During my experiences most of these orgasms happen together, but some women have experienced one without the other. The full body orgasms consist of the woman body jerking uncontrollable. When this happen there's no reason to continue to penetrate her staying inside her while her body shakes is something pleasurable to watch.

Now I will help you understand how squirting and full body orgasms works and the techniques needed to produce these powerful orgasms. The most important things to remember are these orgasms become difficult to produce when the woman is not relaxed. That's why it's important to get her in the orgasmic mind frame and to pose as a sexual threat. Being a sexual threat is simply having confidence and dominance so she feels a vibe that she's able to trust and feel comfortable with you exploring her body. I've explained the importance of confidence and playing the dominant role throughout this book, so you should have a clear idea of how important it is to have these characteristics. When it comes to sex I believe it should always be performed with a purpose, a purpose that both individual reach an unbelievable climax, but most important to satisfy your partner. I stated earlier lesbians are the best at making sure their partner is satisfied first. It may sound strange to some but it's what pushes women more and more in becoming intimate with another woman. One myth people believe when it comes to women dating women is that a woman knows what another woman wants. Well I'm here to tell you that is not always true because there are plenty of women who don't understand the spots that need to be stimulated to create powerful orgasms. Understanding the female body parts are the most important factor when giving women squirting and full body orgasms. As a lesbian I've strived to learn everything possible about the female body to become successful in producing electrifying orgasms.

The first spot I will explore that's the most common which is the G-spot. Most lesbians are familiar with this spot and use it a lot to create intense orgasms. The G-spot is about 1 to 2 inches inside the female vagina on the front wall. Unlike men we as lesbians use our fingers a lot more to build anticipation and to get women to cum, what's so unique about this that most people don't understand is that the fingers can create the same amount of pleasure as a penis. When we as lesbians stimulate the G-spot there are different techniques we use. Remember all the techniques we use cause the woman to have full body and squirting orgasm. Before we stimulate her G-spot we create anticipation by massaging her inner walls then we attack the G-spot. Once she's aroused the index finger is inserted about two inches inside of her with the finger on the front wall and then the G-spot is stimulated using the come here motion, as if you are signaling some one to come here. It's always important to start slow and then build speed. Another technique use on the G-spot is inserting the index and middle finger using the same come here motion but alternating each finger. If you don't get it think about doing the running man with your fingers inside her pussy. When her G-spot tightens on your finger or penis and it becomes difficult to penetrate her you will know you are seconds away from her experiencing a vaginal orgasm.

Just like the G-spot the PS-Spot which is known as the Perineal spot is located about 1 to 2 inches inside the vagina, but located on the rear wall. The PS-spot lies between the vagina and rectum just beneath the perineum (the perineum is the brand of skin between the vaginal opening and the anus). The perineal sponge is a mass of erectile tissues, when stimulated it fills with blood and becomes engorged like the clitoris. The same technique as the G-spot is used to give women an intense orgasm, but pressure is applied in the opposite direction (on the rear wall).

The second spot that's not so common is the D-Spot which is commonly known as the Deep Spot. Most women don't know this spot exist but it can create the most pleasurable orgasm a woman can feel. This is the spot lesbians explore that causes women to go crazy. Stimulating the D-spot correctly caused the woman to experience this pleasurable feeling throughout her body and causes her body to become tense and jerk uncontrollably. The D-Spot is located about 4 to 5 inches inside the woman vagina on the front wall. If you take your middle finger insert it in her vagina along the front wall as far as it would possible go. You would know when you hitting the D-spot when you reached the smooth part of her vagina, you would go from a spongy area to a smooth area. Once you feel the smooth area you are at the D-spot. Unlike the G-spot the D-spot is sensitive all the way around. You can twist you finger and massage the entire D-spot all the way around. This will give the woman a pleasurable sensation that's capable of producing full body orgasms. The D-spot is also similar to the G-spot, pleasure is also felt when the D-spot is stimulated with the come here motion. When her pussy begins to tighten and it becomes difficult to penetrate her she is seconds away from a vaginal orgasm.

Similar to the D-spot the A-spot is located about 4 to 5 inches inside the woman vagina on the rear wall. The A-spot is a little farther to reach than the D-spot being that it's a little deeper on the rear wall. The A-spot can be stimulated just like the D-spot, but pressure is applied in the opposite direction.

The third spot most people are unfamiliar with is the U-spot. The U-spot is commonly known as the urethra, this is the area in which females urinated from. This area is very sensitive and when stimulated it gets as sensitive as the clitoris and can be as pleasurable as the clitoris orgasm. The best way to stimulate this area is by applying moderate pressure with a finger or tongue in a circular motion.

Knowing where these spots are located plays a major role in getting a woman to experience multiple orgasms. Although there are several techniques used to stimulate these spots I used the most basic techniques to give you an idea of how some lesbians make sex so pleasurable with one another. The next chapter will show varies of techniques that lesbians use during sex to create squirting and full body orgasms. Studies have shown more than sixty percent of women never reach orgasms from intercourse alone, and I believe that's true because most people won't take the time out to learn the female body parts. I wasn't always great at sex, but I was determine to learn and I eventually mastered the techniques, applied them with the women I slept with and had great success.

Sexing her the Right Way

Sex with women should be more than thrusting back and forth as hard as you can, while thinking you are beating that pussy up. Stop right there! Many guys have this mentality and I'm here to tell them they have it all wrong. Pounding your dick in and out of her pussy, while you listen to her scream, and then watch her fall out on the bed saying she can't take anymore isn't the orgasm you assume it to be. Here's where men get cocky and brag to their homeboys how they beat that pussy up. They go on and on telling them how she was screaming out loud and how they responded by fucking her until she said she couldn't handle anymore. See I've had this conversation with some of my guy friends on numerous occasions and I laugh at them because they really feel they have put it down. I always ask them is that all, and they respond, "What you mean is that all?" I fucked her until her body couldn't take anymore. I continue to laugh at them because they surely don't understand what squirting and full body orgasms are, and then I start wondering how their women felt during the process. This is where I come to the conclusion that most of these women don't understand their bodies, so I put them in the category with the sixty percent of women who never experienced an orgasm during intercourse. Women who understand their body wouldn't allow a man to pound his dick in and out of her pussy, because she understand when this happen he is hitting her cervix which is painful and causes her to say she can't take anymore. The first thing one must understand during sex is the mental state of the woman and the different spots women are aroused by, which we discussed in the previous chapter. Once that has been established the goal is to stimulate all her spots so that her body becomes familiar with the sensation. Most of the women I've encountered sexually had not experienced squirting and full body orgasms before I came along. All of these women had to be trained and I used different techniques which I'm going to explain in a moment to give them the most incredible experiences of their lives. The techniques I'm about to explain aren't in any particular order, I use these different techniques during sex to give women pleasurable orgasms. The first spot I'm going to discuss is the clitoris. This is the most common spot and is often stimulated with the mouth or hands. When using the hands, I use the squeeze and feather light technique during the romance stage to build the woman's anticipation.

The squeeze consists of grabbing, squeezing and moving the folds of skin that cover and are directly around the clitoris so the clit is sandwiched between these folds of skin. This means you'll never be directly touching her clitoris. You'll be doing this with your thumb and forefingers. When you squeeze these folds of skin between your fingers, you'll be able to feel the pressure it puts on her clit. It feels really good! While keeping the folds of skin firmly between your fingers, start to move your hand from side-to-side or even up and down. Doing this will cause great sensation.

The feather light is really easy and kind of the opposite of the squeeze technique. When using feather light, you are going to be using an absolute minimum amount of pressure on her clit, almost to the point where it will feel more like soft vibrations. To get set up, she should be laying on her back, rub a small amount of lube or saliva on her clit. Next, bring your finger to the side of her clit so that it's just about touching it. It should feel like a feather is touching the side of it. You shouldn't have your finger covering her entire clitoris. Instead it should be just touching the side of it. All you need to do is simply move your finger up and down, while keeping in contact with the side of her clitoris. You will only be moving your finger a few millimeters up and down. So you will hardly be moving it at all. In fact it will feel more like gentle vibrations more than anything else. While doing this, you will notice the tension building and she may start desiring more pressure. If so, don't give in! Keep using only a feather light touch the entire time. This will help to make the whole experience feel like a really long, extended orgasm.

When using the mouth there is really no wrong or right way to eat pussy, everybody has their own style, but there is some do's and don't that come along with it. Next, I will be showing you some amazing techniques that will have her eating from the palm of your hand. The most important thing to remember when eating pussy is to NEVER attack the woman's clitoris from the start. It's crucial to kiss and lick around the clitoris so that anticipation is built. The more anticipation is built the more powerful the orgasm becomes. Once you have licked every inch of her pussy including the labia, perineum, urethra, and vagina, you will know when it's ok to stroke her clit, because she will constantly pull your head towards her clit. This means her clit is throbbing and she's horny as fuck. When you began to stroke her clit with your tongue and you have decided you will be performing intercourse, (for lesbians using the strap) take your index finger and push it in her vagina as far as it would go (with your palm facing down) press down firmly on her A-spot as you eat her pussy. This will cause the ligaments to loose that needs to relax during sex and her vagina will fill with liquids like water running from a hose. This makes her pussy really moist and ready for intercourse without needing lubrication. Continue to press down on her A-spot and eat her pussy until she experience a clitoris orgasm. After giving her a pleasurable clitoris orgasm, one technique I use to get her ready for a vaginal orgasm is the A-spot tap technique.

A-Spot Tap Technique- As her vagina continues to fill with liquids, release her A-spot, insert your middle finger and index finger as far back as they will go with your palm facing down. Start massaging her A-spot in the figure eight motion to get her warmed up. Once you feel she's aroused take the opposite hand and hold down her pelvic bone as you tap her A-spot. Continue to tap her A-spot up and down with pressure until she feels the sensation in the back of her A-spot.

Y-Technique-is used to create a powerful orgasm from the D-spot. Insert your middle and index finger on the front wall (with the palms facing up) as far as they will go without touching her cervix. Spread your middle finger and index finger apart as if you were forming a Y. Once you feel the smooth spongy area you want to apply firm pressure and pull downward. As you continue to pull down on her D-spot, take the opposite hand and press down on her pelvic bone; this will keep her butt from rising off the bed. This technique can cause a powerful orgasm she will feel deep within.

The Bull Horn-causes the G-spot to swell and the female usually responds with a squirting orgasm. Insert the ring and middle finger in her vagina, while your pinky and index finger rest on her labium major (outside her vagina). Continuously pull down on her G-spot using firm pressure to cause her to squirt. Another simple technique you can use on her G-spot is the one finger technique. First you insert your index or middle finger in the woman vagina; once you come in contact with her G-spot you stimulate it by pressing firmly on her G-spot and rubbing it in a circular motion. This will also cause her to squirt.

The V technique- is also known as the vacuum technique which consists of oral and vaginal intercourse. During oral sex, insert your index and middle finger as far as they will go, reaching the D-spot with your palms up. Spread them apart in her vagina forming a V and thrust your finger back and forth, while your chin rest on your palm and your mouth cover her clitoris while you suck it. This will cause her to lose her mind; she will feel the sensation of an oral and vaginal orgasm.

All these techniques are used to get the female familiar with her body; it shows us what her body responds to and how her body should respond when we engage in sex. When these techniques are used correctly you will discover her vagina clamping down on your finger. Once her body responds to these techniques you will become familiar with what's taking place during sex and began to distinguish full body orgasms from squirting orgasms. These techniques are used during the romance stage and are a guide to show what parts of the woman vagina should be stimulated during intercourse. So when a male thrust his dick in and out of a woman vagina he should be pounding on her G-spot, A-spot, or D-spot, not her cervix. Sex is suppose to be pleasurable not painful, so if one claims to have beaten her pussy up, they will clearly be familiar with squirting and full body orgasms. They will also distinguish the difference between a woman saying I can't take it anymore when it's just that damn GOOD and when it's just that damn painful.

The Eight Categories in the Lesbo System

Earlier I spoke of the eight categories women fall into when lesbians are making the decision if the woman they desire will engage in the homosexual lifestyle. In the lesbian system all women fall under one of the eight categories and sometimes develop more than one throughout their romantic adventure. These eight categories are always in the subconscious mind of lesbians, and are used to determine what type of woman they are getting involved with. Most women will engage in the lifestyle but are not willing to commit themselves; most lesbians are ok with this because it's satisfying knowing they are capable of getting the woman they desired. These women are identified in the system as full blown, closet, secretive, curious, bisexual, try-out, not happening, or it just happen woman. During my journey living the lesbian lifestyle I've had encounters with each of these individuals and I tell you if a woman falls in any other category outside these eight, she's probably a transvestite.

The first type of woman is the full blown woman, guys she is exactly that so give up following her around asking for her phone number, and trying to convince her you have the power to change her, you are wasting your time. I have three words for you (it's not happening). The full blown lesbian is one who's attracted to the same sex and the same sex only. She probably has never been with a male and would tell you she was born a lesbian. Most of the full blown women have been attracted to women from the time they distinguish the two genders. It's not quite known why women develop these feelings, but some of these women have suffered from sexual, physical, and mental abuse by a male at a young age and never fully recovered emotionally. These women have developed a hardened attitude towards men and play the role as hard manner to keep the attention from males away. Guys some of these women are fearful and feel you want to take advantage of them so they tell you they don't need a male in their life and that they are content with who they have become.

The second type is the Closet woman, some of these women are able to be identified and some are not. These women are afraid to come out to their family and peers, due to the harsh criticism they may receive, and feel they may be rejected. In many cases, these individuals live their entire life making others believe they are happy when they are not. Some of these women find male companions and live their lives in fear because they feel society labels them as unworthy individuals. Others may play the role as if they can't find a decent male worth their time and uses work as an excuse not to date. They are always complaining about there are no good males and they may be single for a long time. The other women may act as if they love guys, but you never see them with a male companion, they usually have a close girl friend or friends they hang with and they probably have develop a closer relationship then you think. Guys in some cases you can identify if this is your woman, if she seems to be stressed a lot about your relationships, if she doesn't want to engage in any sexual activities, or if she only wants you to perform oral sex instead of vaginal intercourse, and especially if she has a lot of lesbian friends and seems extremely happy when they are around. The Closet woman usually has sexual relations with someone she's comfortable with it may be a close friend who's in a heterosexual relationship or single. They use the heterosexual friend to remain undercover. The Closet woman never wants to be exposed she constantly struggles trying to find ways to open the door and come out.

This runs us into the next woman who's the secretive one. This woman is similar to the closet lady but develops an agreement with her partner. The secretive woman is usually an aggressive, confident, but manipulative individual who develop relationships with the same sex without ever being exposed. These individuals are unique and know how to control the relationship and their partner's mind so things never get out of hand. So guys be careful women can be very sneaky, most of the times these are the women who are married or involved in a committed relationship. The secretive women often times get involved with someone close to her. The individual she deals with is very trustworthy and understand their relationship will always and forever be undercover. These are the girlfriend's which guys suspect nothing more than a friendship. The two share a great deal of intimacy and use parties, outings and vacations for sexual purposes. Guys don't get bent out of shape this is not all women, I'm just exposing those that takes advantage. On the other hand, I have to give the ladies their props who engage in this lifestyle without ever being exposed or jeopardize their relationship with their companion. These women are never exposed because they respect their partner enough to keep it a secret, and understand the relationship they share will never be more than an intimate relationship. The secretive woman usually is able to balance her relationship and affair. In rare cases, their companion may suspect them having an affair with another woman, but never really inquire about it because they truly believe their companion would never engage in the homosexual lifestyle.

The fourth category in the lesbo system is the curious woman. She is the one who has been exposed to the lifestyle by seeing homosexuals in their environment, close family members or friends apart of the homosexual life style. This often times trigger the mind, and gets the woman asking that same question everyone ask, what does two women do? She would then playfully use close friend or family who's exposed to the lifestyle to inquire about the lifestyle, and then make a conscious decision that she's interested in women. Many of these women would front and say they aren't interested in women and will tell others they would never engage in the lifestyle, when their mind constantly wonder what the lifestyle is like. On another note you have the curious woman who just lust for another woman, but never build the confidence to engage in the lifestyle. Sometimes these individuals would partake in the lifestyle and sometimes they remain curious about it.

The fifth category is the bisexual the woman that everyone is familiar with. She's open to both genders and usually is straight forward with her partners. The Bisexual woman is the most complicated for homosexual women to deal with due to the woman wanting the opposite sex at some point. It is much easier for the heterosexual male to deal with these individuals.

Then you have a try-out, this woman is usually an open minded individual who's filled with confidence and understands her sexuality. She will not consider herself a homosexual or bisexual because she will only try the affair to say she tried it out. This is the spontaneous individual who knows she love guys and guys only. She's different from the curious individual because she never wonders about the lifestyle. She simply does it because she wants to. These individuals never commit themselves to the homosexual lifestyle; they do it once and call it quits. They feel they have nothing to hide and will tell to be honest with their companion if asked.

The next type of woman I include in the lesbo system that shouldn't be included is the, it's not happening woman. I included these women because I have personally tried and tried to break these women with different methods and nothing works. So guys just like the full blown lesbians, there are women who will not and I say will not partake in this lifestyle. I usually joke and kid around with my friends and say 99.5% percent of women will sleep with another woman but it's clear to me that more than 5% of women will not sleep with another woman. Basically the hell no it's not happening woman will not bite the bullet no matter how much you charm them. They usually are females who are in serious relationships, married and know that they can not and will not step outside their boundaries. These individuals usually look at the homosexual lifestyle as a disgrace, and abide by the morals and values that were instilled in them at a young age. Most of these individuals do not engage in this lifestyle based on their religious beliefs as well. Their faith is their code of honor and they never engage in a lifestyle that will deter them from their beliefs. Most of these women do not associate nor have friends that live the homosexual lifestyle. Their famous quote is a woman will not and can not do anything for me.

The last type of woman that falls into the lesbo system is the, it just happened woman. These women never intend to have a romantic encounter with another woman. They are usually women who have never thought about having sexual relations with another woman. Sometimes these women are married, or they may be that single woman who's mainly focused on their career and finances. These women are usually lured into the lifestyle by their close friends or homosexuals that live next to them, work with them, etc. the it just happened woman pays no attention and never gets the idea that she's being charmed. They may receive different gifts or invites to outing until they are lured into doing something they had no intentions doing. The it just happen woman is usually a woman who has a soft compassionate side. These types of women never have intentions of being in a relationship with a female, but sometimes if the experience is good they find themselves living the homosexual lifestyle. In other cases these individuals end close friendships because they feel they were taken advantage of.

LESBO EXPERIENCES

Over a course of living the lesbian lifestyle I have observed and encountered several romantic relationships with each type of these women. Some who were in serious relationships, and others who were married. Most of my relationships with these women have been quite adventurous, some were exposed and others still remain a secret. I must say it has been quite interesting and dangerous at times but I love every moment of it. Throughout this chapter you will see how I use the lesbian system I explained in the previous chapter to get the women I desired. Now it's time to enter my world and explore great sex and unbelievable secrets.

THE CLOSET ENCOUNTER

The first woman I encountered a relationship with was the closet woman. Like all closet women she struggled with coming out because of the fear of rejection. She came from a family who had zero tolerance for homosexual relationships, so that made things extremely difficult for her. I met this beautiful woman about 5 feet 6 inches brown skin, long hair, cute smile with dimples my second year of college, I was apart of the Jackson State basketball team, and that was my main priority. I remember it being the first day we moved into the dormitory and the basketball team had the privilege to move in the honors dormitory. That was a huge move for the team being that we had to stay in McAllister White Side my freshman year. The honors dormitory had suites; its capacity was eight people per suite compared to fifty people per hall in McAllister White side. It was the first day for move in, all the campus members of the basketball team registered and got situated in their rooms. I was fortunate to have had the same roommate as my freshman year, because we never knew if the coaches would pair us with the incoming freshmen. As I enter the suite and began to remove the items from my tote, I notice this young woman coming out of her room, locking her door, with a basketball in her hand. I looked at my roommate and she asked, "Is that one of the freshmen". I shrugged my shoulders and told her I didn't know. The woman exits the suite as if she was going to play basketball. As my roommate and I continued to settle in our room over the course of an hour, we noticed the woman coming back into the suite and my roommate ask me to ask the woman if she was a freshmen recruit. Initially I was a bit nervous, for what reason, I don't know but I eventually made my way to this woman and remember saying to myself she looks a bit sophisticated to play basketball. She had an amazing face and physique I would never forget. I was instantly attracted to her when I approached her and proceeded to ask the woman her name and if she was a freshman recruit. She told me her name, and stated, "I'm not a recruit, but I'm looking to try-out for the team". I told her that was cool and she was in the right suite being that my roommate and I was already on the team. I then began to tell her about the team and invited her to some of our scrimmage games we played outside of practice. I knew this would be a way to enter the friend zone and to potentially develop an intimate relationship, but I wasn't quite sure how that would go. She eventually showed up at some of our scrimmage games and after one particular scrimmage I treated her to some food at a local diner to become more acquainted. During our outing she opened up and began to tell me how she felt home sick being eight hundred miles away from home, and how she missed her family, some of her friends, and her boyfriend of four years. Hearing the word boyfriend made me a bit uncomfortable, but it dawned on me that he was eight hundred miles away. After eating at the diner and making small talk we went back to the dormitory and continued our conversation in my room. Over a course of weeks we became closer and I began to notice my roommate wasn't spending much time on campus and her roommate

decided to withdraw from school so
that allowed us to spend even more
time with each other. We stayed up
countless nights in each other rooms
talking, laughing, and even watching
movies; we always departed from each
other when we felt tired and sleepy,
until this Thursday night. I left her
room around eleven o'clock, we had
class early the next morning and we
thought we had enough fun for one
night. I'll never forget this night we
enjoyed each other company to the
point a bond was formed and both of
us felt it. I didn't want to leave and she
didn't want me to go, but we knew we
needed to attend the classes we had the
next day because we had missed them
the prior two weeks. When I got to my
room I undressed to my boxers and t-
shirt, then I laid down. I remember
telling myself I was in control and I
had the one woman that brightened my

day, in my corner. About twenty minutes passed and I heard a knock at the door. I got up a bit agitated because I knew my roommate had her key because she had to use it to get in the front door. When I opened the door there she stood with her short shorts and this beautiful smile on her face, and then said in a soft tone with her lips poked out, "I'm scared". I remember smiling and asking her, scared of what? She replied, "Of the dark, can you stay with me tonight". We both smiled and starred in each other eyes; we knew exactly what we wanted to happen. I left my room crept in her room, due to our nosey suite mates, laid in the vacant bed, from her roommate moving out and started to watch the movie Kingdom Come. I remember lying in the vacant bed because I didn't want to be too aggressive and go right in. We never discussed her being intimate with other women, she always spoke highly of her boyfriend, and I wasn't going to risk my chances with her by being too aggressive. Although we could feel the sexual tension I stayed on the other bed watching TV while giving her that I want to fuck you eye. She eventually recognized the eye and said, "Why are you over there"? I asked her where you want me to be, and she replied, "Over here with me". I eventually got up and moved to her bed. I wanted to be in the dominate position so I lay down behind her with my arm around her waist. She didn't ask me what I was doing, so I figured she was comfortable with my actions We continued to watch the movie; nothing was progressing so I used the I'm asleep tactic to get her attention. When she rolled over and noticed I was asleep; she pat me in the face and quoted from the movie, "Wake up Hud". I opened my eyes as If I was asleep gazed directly in her eyes and the forward motion began. Our lips met and we began to kiss passionately, we twirled our tongues in and out of each other mouths as intensity began to build. She whispered I'm a virgin, so make this special. Different emotions ran through my body like electricity, because I understood this was a special moment, not because she never experienced this, but because she trusted me with her body. I whispered to her I have nothing but good intentions and I'm going to cherish your body and this moment for the rest of my life, and I promised her nothing will hurt and told her to relax her mind and ordered her to tell me what she wanted me to do to her, and how she wanted me to make her feel. As she began to whisper make me feel like I never felt before, I lightly licked her lips and our tongues became tangled and began to twirl in each other mouth. As I glanced at her I knew she was lost in the moment so I began to kiss behind her ear, down her neck and on to her collarbone. Her body began to jerk from the soft kisses and she began to moan make love to me. I moved from her collar bone to her breast and licked around and under her breast as her nipples sprouted out like small raisins. Moving from her right breast to the left, I licked her nipples like ice cream from a cone. I started from the base, licked my way to the top, and sucked her nipples like sucking ice cream right off the top. I gently pressed both breast together and sucked her nipples firmly. She moaned, became more relaxed and whispered I love you. I didn't know what to say I was lost for words and had to believe her because I was the first person she trusted. Apparently her boyfriend didn't build that much closeness for her to engage in this act with him. I whispered I love her back because that's exactly how I felt; I reminisced over the course of weeks and remembered my feelings had become involved and I knew I loved her. As I reflected on my feelings I moved from her breast, down her stomach, to her pelvic area, then to her inner thigh. I gently kissed her inner thigh made my way to her pussy and began to lick softly around her clit. Moisture build and her clit became hard as a cherry on a stem, and I had every intention to suck it that way. I continued to lick in and around her pussy as she grabbed my head pressing it towards her clit. I wasn't going in just yet, anticipation was the key, and I wanted her to feel the sensation from me eating her pussy the right way. As I licked every part around her clit from the labia to the inner walls down to the perineum then back up to the urethra. She continued to moan and press my head towards her clit. I realized how much anticipation I had built, so I stroked her swollen clit with my tongue and recognized how it sent her body into shock. She pressed my head even harder wanting me to lick her clit to send that intensity through her body again. Then I realized it was time to go in and make her feel the emotions she never felt. I then began to lick from her urethra to her clit like I had to catch the juices running from an apple. When I reached the top I sucked her clit firmly which caused her body to shake like a seizure patients. As I licked and sucked her clit at the same time, her body seized, as I continued the motion she moaned louder, and pushed my head back when she reached the orgasmic state. I realized she couldn't take any more, so I slowly kissed my way up her body, to her mouth and noticed she was shedding tears. I asked her if I had done something wrong, she replied, "I never felt this way before". Tears flowed tremendously, and I was there to comfort her. I wiped the tears from her face as I told her I loved her. Unexpectedly she told me my job wasn't finished. Wanting to make this a special encounter I never had the intention of penetrating her, as tears flowed and she repeated my job wasn't finished I kissed her until chills covered our bodies. I gently rubbed inside her pussy in a circular motion until my index finger was inserted in her pussy. To keep the tension from her pussy I continued to kiss her passionately as I reached her G-spot. I then softly stroked her G-spot with a come here motion while she moaned immensely. Her moans soothe my body like music to my ears. I remember looking at the clock, the time was 1:47 a.m., we had been making love over an hour and a half, and things had just become heated. As I continued to stroke her G-spot, I decided to go a little further to her D-spot and realized things were a bit tighter. I didn't want to rush things and most importantly I didn't want her to experience pain. So I gently broke through the barriers and began to massage her D-spot her moans became more intense and she began to experience the pleasure of penetration. As I continued to massage her D-spot firmly, I kissed and sucked her breast to make the experience that much more pleasurable. After several minutes she experienced a vaginal orgasm that cause her body to shake uncontrollably, I wrapped the night up with a fontal lobe kiss and we cuddled the night away. If you're wondering, we didn't make it to class the next morning, but we did realize she was no longer a virgin. Over the next couple days, which were the weekend, she avoided me by staying in her room with the door closed. I was emotionally frustrated because I didn't know what type of emotions she was experiencing after our sexual encounter. That Sunday I knocked on her door, she opened it, I asked her if she was ok, we talked and she explained how she felt emotionally and later that night we continued where we had left off early Friday morning. We eventually developed an incredible bond and began a three year relationship. It took a while before she told her parents, but she slowly made her way out of the closet.

THE SECRECTIVE ENCOUNTER

The secretive woman was quite a challenge for me; there were several encounters where she could have been exposed but her creative mind during difficult times saved her. It all began at the job. It was her first day on the job and I noticed the negative attitude she had towards me from the start. I had never seen someone who expressed so much anger towards a person they didn't know. I then began to realize she expressed this hatred because of my lifestyle and I couldn't understand it because my lifestyle had nothing to do with her. I was determined to change her perception of homosexuals, I knew it would be a tough task but I was up for the challenge. As we worked closer and closer each day I eventually had the opportunity to work with her hands on. As the day passed we sat and talked and enjoyed each other conversation and it turned out I wasn't so bad after all. It all began May 9th, me and my best friend were returning from Memphis Tennessee when I received an unexpected phone call from her. The conversation was short, but it caught me by surprise because I never expected her to call. After working with her for a while I knew we where in a better place and I had felt there was some type of attraction between the both of us. Things had already been confirmed for me when a mutual friend told me the two of them had a conversation about me during a trip they had taken, but she had no idea we discussed their conversation. Later that evening of May 9th I received another phone call by surprise and the conversation wasn't so short we talked for hours and the conversation became more intimate as the night progressed. Several weeks had past and our bond was growing immensely, I was dating at the time and she was in a committed relationship herself. I was in love with my partner at the time, but I let the attraction overcome my love, and eventually fell in love with her. As things progressed I knew she was still uncomfortable with my lifestyle and I knew going out would make things a little more difficult, but I asked her out anyway. We eventually had a couple of outings and she enjoyed herself. Our first romantic encounter came when she asked me to go out of town with her. I was a bit hesitant at first because I knew things could get a bit heated and she would be exposed to something she had never been apart of. Finally, I gave in and decided to take the trip. We planned the trip one early morning after my work night, so I could avoid going home having to explain to my partner my plans. We were already on bad terms and she had assumed I was having an affair with someone else, so I packed my bag the previous day before work, so I could be ready when I got off. After completing my shift, I parked my car at the nearest Wal-Mart and out of town we went. When we reached our destination, she was excited about shopping and I was under the impression she was going to take me to a hotel where I would shower then enjoy the pleasure of shopping, but things didn't go as I planned. She stopped at the first shopping mall and began shopping, I became frustrated and a bit annoyed because I had worked the night shift and wanted to shower before I started any other

activities. I guess she felt going to the
hotel would open things up sexually
and she wasn't ready for that, although
she talked big about us being intimate
the night before. After a period of time
she realized how frustrated I had
become so she decided to take me to
the nearest hotel, which was the
Holiday Inn Express. I didn't want her
to feel as if sex was on my mind, so I
told her to stay in the car while I
showered. I exit the car with my bag,
entered the hotel to check in and by
surprise she was behind me. I
reminded her she didn't have to get out
and told her I didn't want to make her
uncomfortable, but she insisted she
was not staying in the car. As I entered
the room I turned on the television
began to undress to my boxer and t-
shirt and headed to the bathroom. After
showering I exit the bathroom to put
on my clothes and I noticed her lying

under the cover. I sat on the other bed and noticed her Tommy Hilfiger jeans were lying across the bed, I got up pulled the covers from off her and we began to tussle with the covers, which lead to us wrestling and ended with our tongues. This immediately began to change as our tongues collided with one another I tried to put my hands in her panties but she gripped them so tight as if she was a virgin who was experiencing sex for the first time. I then began to tell her to relax and that I wasn't going to do anything to hurt her, she became relaxed and I made my way inside her panties and noticed the wetness of her pussy. As I massaged her clit, she released the grip on her panties and I began to pull them off. Her breathing became heavy as I kissed my way down her body, and started to eat her pussy like her man never done. Her breathing and moaning became intense as I licked from her perineum to her clitoris. Her juice flowed heavily as I sucked her clit and my tongue fucked her pussy, she reached the climax and I noticed her body trembling uncontrollably. We laid around afterwards and then checked out the hotel. I knew things were difficult for her to grasp because this was the first time she slept with someone outside her marriage, and to make matters worst she slept with a woman. On the way back from our trip she sobbed uncontrollably and I felt guilty, because I felt I took advantage of her. I started to wonder if I forced myself on her when she was gripping her panties. When we made it back in town, she dropped me off at Wal-Mart where my car was parked and we parted ways. We didn't speak the next couple of days, but we eventually seen each other at work and she was still upset about what had happen. We talked about the situation and formed a bond that would never be broken. We continued our relationship for a few years before we decided to put the intimate side away. Like most secretive women she knows her secret is safe with me and she knows we've build trust that her marriage is never in jeopardy. We both understand that the intimacy we once shared will always and forever remain undercover. We have had our share of problems, but we remain close and will always hold a special place in our hearts for each other.

Secretive Encounter 2

I had the biggest crush on this woman. She had just moved in the apartment complex and I noticed her slim waist, phat ass, and cute face. She had a boyfriend she dated for ten years and he had her ass on lock. When she first moved in it seemed she was stuck up, she never spoke, and acted as if she was too good to socialize with people in the neighborhood, but things changed in 2005. Her boyfriend was locked up for drugs and we experienced the most devastating storm that pulled everyone in the neighborhood together. It was hurricane Katrina, and we suffered without lights and other supplies for weeks. As for myself I tried to make sure the families in the neighborhood weren't suffering, so I felt the need to lift the spirit of those around me. As a community we pulled together and overcame the adversities of hurricane Katrina. A couple of months later, the woman came to me and told me how she loved my courageous act during the storm and we became close thereafter. I knew I had showed that likeable personality and figured I was getting closer to an intimate relationship with her. We started communicating over the phone night after night for hours and I began to realize I was getting even closer to a sexual encounter, until her boyfriend got out of jail. Our conversation immediately ceased and I respected that because I didn't want to put her relationship in jeopardy. Besides she had dated this guy for ten years and I knew through our phone conversation she loved this man despite the trouble he constantly got in. Although we didn't get to talk on the phone as much, when we saw each other we could tell we wanted to fuck, and we knew we would have to sneak around to do it. One evening I was sitting around the house and received a phone call. She had called me to let me know her boyfriend was going to Atlanta that night with some of his friends, and wanted to know if I was up for coming over. This kind of caught me off guard because she never invited me over, not even during the countless nights we spent on phone when her boyfriend was locked up. I told her I would come, and she told me to come to her back door around 1:00 a.m. it would be unlocked. She didn't want any of the nosey neighbors noticing she had company, and she surely didn't want her boyfriend to find out about it. I sat around the rest of the evening thinking about the conversations we had when her boyfriend was locked up. I remembered her bragging about how good her pussy was, and how she would have me crying if we ever fucked around. So I started planning how I was going to do things when I got there. I surely wasn't going over weak minded because I knew she was an aggressive, strong headed individual who thought she had some banging ass pussy, but I had one goal and that was to make her cum like she never cum before. When the clock struck 1:00 am I smiled and started to pack my bag. I wasn't going to be on time because I was in control and the last thing I wanted was to look desperate. Around 1:30 am I received a text message that read, where are you? I've been waiting, if you couldn't handle the pussy you should have text me or something. I didn't text back, I left my apartment walked to her apartment and like she said the back door was unlocked. When I walked in candles was lit and you could smell the vanilla fragrance. She was laying on the couch naked with a robe thrown over her, so I walked up to her and noticed she had an attitude because I was late, but I didn't say anything I snatched the robe off her and starred at her body while biting my bottom lip with my eyes tight and admired how the complexion of her skin appeared silky smooth, her small perky breast, her slim waist line, round phat ass, and how pretty her pussy looked from her fresh bikini wax. Without saying a word, she looked at me with anger and I started kissing her body all over. The attitude she had quickly left and she ask me that's how you feel? I responded this is long over due. We made our way to the bedroom where things got extremely freaky I started licking her manicured toes and rubbing her legs. I realized I started things off with this woman like I was in love with her, but I knew that wasn't the case I knew I had a point to prove from all the conversations we had, and I wasn't about to back down. As I sucked her toes I made my way up her inner thigh and realize I was giving her a little too much in the beginning so I started to slow things down. I got up, looked at her as she smiled and talked shit, I turned on the radio and noticed she had a slow jam CD in the player. Instead of playing the radio I played the CD, removed the grape seed oil from my bag, returned to the bed and massaged her body all over. I knew anticipation is always the key to great sex and that was my intention. Her mind became more relax from the massage and her body language screamed fucked me. She was laying on her back so I kissed down her back, her butt, down her thighs, and began to kiss and lick her pussy and ass, as she rose up in the doggy style position, her legs spread wider and she screamed fuck me. Her pussy was drenching with the juices that ran from the inside, I laid under her as she straddled my face and inserted two fingers in her pussy and pushed down on the front wall of her D-spot while sucking her clit. Her moans became intense and she screamed I'm about to cum, I sucked harder and started finger fucking the back wall of her D-spot she moaned that feels good I can feel it in my ass, and her body immediately began to jerk uncontrollable. She fell down on the bed and said damn you do know what you're doing don't you. I never had my pussy ate like that. I kissed her and things began to heat up again so I aggressively pulled her to the edge of the bed, placed a pillow under her butt, held her legs open with my arms, put my dick in her pussy and fucked her until she squirted all over me and the bed. When she experienced that squirting orgasm I knew my job was done and I knew it was a success. I couldn't stay too much longer because I knew the sun was coming up and I had to get home before the nosey ass neighbors saw me. So I got up to put on my clothes, and she grabbed me pulled me on the bed and said damn I wasn't expecting that from you, meet me here the same time tomorrow. Our relationship lasted about five months. She ended up moving after the police raided her apartment during a drug bust and her boyfriend was sentenced to 7 years in prison behind that shit. She ended up marrying some other guy, but she's still living a secret life with her best friend.

THE BISEXUAL ENCOUNTER

I became acquainted with the bisexual woman through a social networking site Myspace; she was a very attractive young woman, about five feet five inches, long hair, light skin, with a petite frame. One particular evening I was designing my Myspace page when I received a message in my inbox from her asking me my name and she admitted right off she was bisexual. We eventually developed a great friendship, although I was in a relationship with the girl of my dreams. I continued to communicate with this female on a friend level as my relationship was slowly ending, due to the lack of time me and my partner were spending together. I worked at Wal-Mart overnight, attended classes in the morning, and attended track practice in the evening. The only free time I had came when I didn't have track meets on the weekend, my girlfriend constantly complained about the time we never spent together, so we drifted apart and she became involved in an intimate relationship with someone else. She had no idea I was aware of her dating someone else. We lived together and shared the same computer for school purposes. One day she got careless and forgot to logout of her email and I was exposed to numerous emails written between her and her new friend. I wasn't upset about it because I knew our relationship was falling apart due to the lack of time we got to spend. I decided to invest the little time I did have in this woman I met on Myspace. We became closer and since she wasn't dating at the time we decided to develop an intimate relationship. I didn't pay much attention to my girlfriend thereafter, I was out to get revenge and I wanted her to feel pain. When I found out my girlfriend was spending the night on campus with her new girlfriend I decided to invite my friend to the house and fill it with nothing but pleasure. I knew my girlfriend routine so I planned things perfectly. She would always spend the night on campus and come home early in the morning before I returned from work to get dressed for school, as if I had no idea of what she was doing. So this particular night I called in from work, got dressed as if I was heading to work, left home, parked my car across the street and I noticed my friend leaving home. I trailed her to the campus watched her enter the dormitory and then I left to pick up my friend from her house. We drove back to my house, I lit some candles, fixed her a meal she enjoyed, which consisted of grilled ranchero chicken and potatoes, steamed broccoli and green salad, we drank a bottle of blackberry merlot wine. She was impressed and I could see it in her eyes she was ready to fuck. I left the room went to the bathroom put on my dick and the night began. When I came out she was lying in the bed naked playing with her pussy as she gave me an eye that said come fuck me. I knew my girlfriend had a key and could pop up at any moment but that was the least of my worries, my focus was on fucking her brains out. I went over to the bed pushed her back and began to kiss her inner thigh, while I gently grabbed her breast and squeezed them to her nipples hardening. As I kissed her thighs and around her pussy she screamed fuck me. I inserted my middle finger and started stroking her G-spot and noticed her pussy soaked, she was horny and wanted to feel some pressure, so I finger fucked her until her G-spot swelled, then I put my dick in her pussy and fucked her until her pussy gripped my rubber dick and pushed it out, juices squirted from her pussy like a water hose. I wasn't finish just yet I wanted her to feel the orgasm through her body, so I laid on the bed she straddled me and the ride began. She rode my dick for several minutes without experiencing the full body orgasm, so I knew off top she wasn't use to getting fucked in the right places. So I immediately pushed my dick about five to six inches inside her pussy on the front wall and began to fuck her with all the pressure on her front wall. As I pumped hard stimulating her G-spot and D-spot at the same time she fell back off my dick and began to squirm like a fish without water. As her body shook uncontrollable I watched her experience her first vaginal orgasm, she eventually dosed off and I knew I had to get her home before my girlfriend came home. She usually would make it home right before 7:00 a.m. Time passed 4:00a.m. turned into 5:00a.m. and 5:00a.m turned into 6:00a.m. I knew I was pushing it, that's when I acted as If I was late for work. I woke her up and told her I was late for work and need to get her home. She woke up, in a hurry, began to get dress and apologized for making me late. We left my house around 6:30 a.m. and my girlfriend was nowhere in sight, I felt relieved since I escaped the scene without putting my friend in danger. I dropped my friend off and returned home around 8:00a.m. I figured my girlfriend had been home and left for school as usual. When I drove up to the house I noticed my friend car wasn't outside, so I figured she had come home and left. When I entered the house, I noticed I left the wet sheets on the bed, my dick on the bed, and the candles lit. Before I could clean up my mess my girlfriend walked in and noticed the dick we used lying around. She became upset, and started to scream at me and ask why I fucked another bitch in our house. Things became very physical, she called the police, and instead of taking me to jail they made me leave the house. I later returned to get my clothes another dispute happened which lead the police to come and I never returned after that. I developed an intimate relationship with my Myspace friend until my ex-girlfriend found out and ended up jumping on her after a few months. I must say the revenge was sweet. I no longer communicate with my first love, but I

still run across my Myspace friend on
several occasions and we remain good
friends.

Bisexual Encounter 2

This particular woman I've
known for quite a while now, although
our relationship didn't last she would
always have a special place in my
heart. When I first noticed her I
admired the classiness about her so
that was an instant attraction for me. I
couldn't quite figure out where to put
her in the eight categories when I first
met her, so I decided to fall back and
let things play out on their own. As
time went by, I decided not to
approach her instead I chose to let the
likeable characteristic draw her in, and
that's exactly what happened. She
eventually approached me and asked if
I like to read books. I told her yeah, so

she told me to stop by the library one day and see her. At that moment I knew I wanted to visit her, but I was in a relationship and didn't want to put my relationship in jeopardy so I didn't respond. Days passed and I couldn't help but think about her and want to take my chances by going to visit her at the library. My relationship with my girlfriend eventually became rocky; I guess I got tired of dealing with the fact that she was a flight attendant. The time away from home seemed a bit too much for me after meeting this new woman. After picking a fight, I went to the library where she worked and we sat and talked until the library closed; I was amazed at the conversation. There was an emotional connection and surely attraction was there. I started visiting her everyday at library until one day things got heated. Usually I would go there to have a conversation, but we felt well aquatinted and fucking was on our minds. She told me to meet her in the restroom, so I went to the restroom where she stood. We entered the handicap stall I pulled down her pants, she sat on the handicap rail open her legs and I notice she was prepared. Her fresh bald pussy was moist and ready for my tongue to take over. I started kissing her as she got lost in the moment I went down and my soft lips met her pussy and the scent of coconut verbena hit my nose. The scent aroused me in ways that lead me to licking every inch of her pussy and ass. I open her pussy wide licked all around as her eyes rolled in her head. I didn't wear my dick because I had no idea we was going to get freaky in the library. Instead I fucked her pussy with my tongue while stimulating her clit as my tongue exit her vagina. I could tell by her reaction she loved the combination of the two. So I inserted my index finger and fucked her pussy as I sucked her clit. She cummed and screamed, "I needed this". She quickly got dressed because she had to get back to work we exit the bathroom continued our conversation until it was time to go. This was our first encounter as partners but had more intense sexual encounters later in our relationship. We dated for years after that, but eventually my wild side came out and I wanted to have an open relationship that she didn't agree with. We grew apart which I regret today, but we communicate from time to time and she has moved on and dating guys again.

IT JUST HAPPEN

She was a close friend who was adamant about her relationship with her long time fiancé. She was attractive and had a body of a goddess. We met through a mutual friend and became friends in the spring of 2008. Although our friendship was a little rocky in the beginning we eventually became close, and I started to develop mixed feelings for her. At times I wanted to explore the intimate side, and other times I felt we developed a solid foundation as friends and I didn't want to deter from that. Before I attempt an intimate relationship with women, I size them up and determine where they fall in the lesbian system. It all boils down to if I feel the woman would or would not be intimate with another woman. I make this decision based on the woman religious views and/or how connected she is with her male companion. With this friend there was no doubt in my mind she loved her fiancé and women wasn't an option. I initially labeled her as the "it's not happening woman". As time went by we became closer and we started to spend a lot of time together. I began to notice we were spending more time than with her fiancé, so I started to analyze the situation and came to the conclusion she and her fiancé were having problems. As a friend, I became concerned and wanted to make sure things were ok with her, but I didn't want to bombard her and make her feel uncomfortable incase she was having problems. So I eventually thought of a way to address the issue without attacking her. I asked her if she was ok, then mentioned how we had been hanging out a lot, and asked her how her fiancé felt about her hanging out a lot". She told me they were having normal relationship issues and that he didn't care; he was hanging out a lot himself. This changed everything, she became open and I began to realize the perfect fiancé wasn't so perfect. I began to get phone calls on a regular on how things were not going well and I stayed up countless of nights giving positive feedback, because I was a friend and I wanted nothing but the best for her. She deserved someone good and I made sure she was aware of that. Late one evening I received a phone call from her and she was hysterical. She told me she and her fiancé got in a heated argument, and she needed to remove herself from the situation and needed somewhere to stay for the night. I agreed, she came over and we discussed the situation in detail. After several hours of conversation, I noticed she became emotionally drained so I offered her my bedroom for rest. As she prepared for bed I started some house duties, when I finish the house duties I laid on the couch and watched television until I heard her crying. I went to the bedroom and asked if she was ok, she wept and begin to tell me how much she loved her fiancé, but felt they were falling apart. I sat on the edge of the bed, and before I knew it I embraced her and assured her that everything was going to be alright. As I consoled her the feelings that were lingering struck me at once. I wrapped my arms around her pulled her closer and kissed her on the frontal lobe. I knew she was in a vulnerable state, but I had no intentions of taking advantage of that. She looked at me with tears in her eyes and asked what the kiss was about. I knew it wasn't the right time to tell her I had developed some feelings over the course of our friendship, instead I told her I felt she was an amazing girlfriend and she was too good of a person to let the situation get her down. I encouraged her to find strength and rise above the situation. She then responded, "That's why I love you". A bit nervous, I stood up and turned to exit the room when she asked if I was coming back, she stated she wasn't sleepy. I told her yes I was going to fix me a drink, and she asked if I would fix her one. After returning with the drinks she laid in the bed as I sat on the edge, we talked and then she asked if I was afraid to get in the bed with her. I stated, "No" and she replied, "Just don't do anything crazy". I laughed and got in the bed. Before I knew it the alcoholic beverages had taken effect, she was emotional again.

Once again I pulled her close with my arms around her and stroked her arm gently as she sobbed. She looked at me and thanked me for letting her stay the night and I told her that's what friends are for. Before I knew it I kissed her frontal lobe and then made my way to her lips. Our tongues were tangled and by surprise she was kissing me back. While things were heated I removed her shirt and began to suck her breast. As her nipples became hard I cupped them with my hand and began to lick around them. I could tell I was building anticipation because she moaned wanting me to suck her nipples. Instead I put my hand in the pajamas she was wearing and began to massage the inner walls of her pussy. Her moans became more intense as I stroked her G-spot and stimulated her clit with my fingers. I continued to lick around her nipples as her body jerk from the ripple effect. I was aiming for a powerful squirting orgasm using the simplest techniques. After several minutes I noticed she was ready to explode so I firmly sucked her nipples and inserted two fingers in her pussy reaching her deep spot. As I stroked her deep spot continuously with the same rhythm and pressure, I could feel her pussy tighten pushing my fingers out of her. I immediately inserted the fingers back in her pussy and stroked her deep spot again. Things became electric she screamed at the top of her lungs as her pussy gripped my fingers and this clear liquid shot from her pussy like a cannon, she soaked the sheets. As we wrapped the night up she told me she never experienced that before and inquired about all the wetness of the sheets. I attempted to explain things to her, but she fell asleep during the lecture. I eventually dosed off, woke up the next morning with a note on my dresser saying last night was beautiful, I experienced something I haven't experienced in thirty years. I will always and forever love your chivalrous character, but I'm committed in making things work with my fiancé and the act of last night was unacceptable. Hopefully you won't take things personally and our friendship will continue. P.S. let's keep this our little secret☺. When I read this letter I couldn't do anything but smile because I realized she was the "it just happened woman", but I was even happier I got to exploit this sexual opportunity. Since then she has ended things with her fiancé and working on a more promising relationship, we continue to remain good friends, but we aren't close as we once were, and have never discussed the sexual encounter we had.

THE TRY-OUT ENCOUNTER

I was close with this woman, but
our friendship fell apart because she knew
exactly what she wanted and nothing was
going to deter her from that. I respected that
because I knew she had a loving boyfriend
who would marry her one day. We became
close friends and hung out every opportunity
we had. She knew I was a lesbian, but she
never seen me interact in that lifestyle
around her. I made sure I didn't jeopardize
our friendship by forcing her to engage in
the homosexual activities I was apart of.
Although she was confident about her
sexuality, she always asked me why I was so
secretive about my lifestyle and wanted to
know why I didn't invite her to some of the
gay events I attended. What she didn't
understand is I wasn't secretive about my
lifestyle, but I knew when I was around her
boyfriend; he was uncomfortable with us
being friends so I thought it wasn't
appropriate to talk about my lifestyle or

invite her to any events because I respected the fact he was against the lifestyle. Our friendship grew over the years and we became closer and went from hanging out three times a week to every day, and that's when things became a problem. What most people in society don't understand is because a heterosexual individual is friends with a homosexual individual don't mean they are engaging in sexual acts. That's exactly what happened in this case. Her boyfriend started to accuse her of messing around with me; no matter how many times she defended herself he constantly accused her. One morning I received a call from my friend she was hysterical, I couldn't understand what she was saying because she was so upset. I then heard a knock at my door and when I opened it, she was standing there with the phone to her ear with tears pouring from her face. I invited her in, we sat in the living room as she pulled herself together and told me her boyfriend said, he didn't want to be in a relationship with her anymore because of our friendship. I was pissed the fuck off because I never understood why people are always bashing gay folks. I had been friends with this woman for six years and was there when she was having a difficult time deciding whether to have their child or an abortion. This really fucked with me emotionally, so I cooked dinner for us. She eventually came around and we discussed the issue over dinner and decided we would end our friendship so her relationship could work. I was disappointed about the decision, but I realized she had a great relationship with her boyfriend and I knew deep in my heart he was a good dude and he loved her more than anything in this world, and I knew she felt the same way. As the day passed we talked about how we would miss each other and tried to decide what we could do to remember each other forever. We thought about getting matching necklaces but we knew we probably weren't going to keep up with them forever. Then we decided on matching tattoo, but we knew if her boyfriend found out he would make a big deal out of it. So she said with a smile, "I have an idea". I told her it better not be anything stupid. She said we can have sex since this will be our last time seeing each other. I responded, "Girl you have lost your mind". She stated, "Why not we will always remember this and you know the memory will last forever". I wasn't down for that because we had been close friends forever and although she was sexy as hell I never had the intentions to fuck around. I realized I had seen this woman naked; I had massaged her back and shoulder after a long day of work, but fucking her was not going to happen. So I told her, "I'm not going to do it, if your boyfriend finds out about this he is really going to be through with your ass". Surprisingly she stated, "How will he", and continued to say "I wanted to try this anyway". I was lost for words and still didn't agree to it. She walked up to me and wrapped her arms around my neck and said, "I don't want to lose you as a friend". I wrapped my arms around her waist tears fell from my eyes and I felt the wetness of my t-shirts from her tears so I grabbed her tighter and started to kiss her on her frontal lobe. When she lifted her head; the tears flowed heavily, she kissed my lips, and said make this special. We began to kiss and every thing felt so right. It seemed as if we had done this before, but I knew this was the first and last time. We made our way to my bedroom. I undressed her pushed her on the bed, reached for the massage oil off the dresser and began massaging her back and shoulder like the times before. As tears flowed from my face, I kissed her back down her butt, between her thighs and tasted her sweet pussy. As I licked her pussy she pressed back on my tongue and back and forth she bounced on my tongue. I was confused about what was going on, but I was going to make the best of the situation. I grabbed my strap from the drawer put it on, placed it between her pussy lips and rubbed it from her perineum to her clit until her pussy was wet. When her pussy was running with juice I put my dick inside her and started pumping her with short strokes until her G-spot started to clamp down on my dick I knew she was ready to cum so I fucked her harder while I placed my thumb on her clit and massage it in a circular motion. Her body lost control and she moaned loud while hitting her fist against the wall. She screamed I don't want you to ever forget this moment" as she pushed me down on my back. She was ready to ride my dick. She straddled me put my dick in her pussy leaned forward and fucked the shit out of me. As her ass bounced up and down I pumped with the motion giving her long strokes, hitting her D-spot she pulled my dreads and rode my dick until her water broke. She had released so much ejaculation the sheets were soaking wet. I wasn't finish with her just yet, after she cum she fell on the bed I pulled her to the edge of the bed opened her legs and ate her pussy like I was in love with her, before I knew it her body was jerking and she was pushing my head away. She couldn't handle anymore. Afterwards we lie in the bed about an hour, cried and reminisce on all the fun times we shared. She eventually got up took a shower got dressed, kissed me and told me thanks for being such a great friend, and left the house. Just like that our friendship ended we stop communicating, she rekindled with her boyfriend they had a baby boy and they are married today. I hate that we had to end our friendship because of something so simple, but I'm still proud of the woman she has become and I would always and forever remember the friendship we once shared.

THE CURIOUS ENCOUNTER

I met the curious woman through a mutual friend who was a straight woman. She invited me to her house warming party where there were so many fine straight women, I damn near felt out of place, but my friend always wanted me to meet her best friend; she had talked highly about her every since we became friends, so I was excited to meet her. When she introduced me to her friend she was snobby. She had an attitude that took away from her good looks. She was about 5'5" pretty brown skin, silky black hair, and her eyes were amazing. When I extended my hand to introduce myself she asked our friend, "Is this the person you always hanging with, are you serious a homo". I responded, "Yes, I'm the homo she hangs with, if there's a problem you can leave". She walked away and the party continued. Because her friend moved to Tupelo, a couple of hours away, they didn't get to spend as much time as they use to. As the party continued, I socialized with several of the women and enjoyed myself. When the house warming party ended I stayed behind to help my friend clean up and of course her best friend stayed as well. She was staying the weekend to hang out with her bestie. While I vacuum the carpet she tapped me on my shoulder and apologized for her action earlier that evening and told me she hope she didn't offend me when she called me a homo. I smiled and told her, "I am a homo and that would never offend me". She then proceeded to ask me how I met her friend and how we became so close. I explained that and also made her aware that my sexuality has nothing to do with being a great friend, nor does it means I like every woman I come in contact with. I told her she can relax around me and not worry about me hitting on her. I made it known that I was a very respectful individual. When I finished cleaning, I told my friend I would let them have their girl time and that I would be in touch with her later the next week. I wanted her to enjoy her time with her best friend. I left and went home but later that night my friend called me telling me her friend wanted me to know how sorry she was. I told my friend, she had already apologized earlier. This gave me the impression that I must have done something that showed I was likeable. What other reason she would have her to call me. I told my friend since she was so apologetic how about she attend Que Delta week with us since we had planned to go the next month. My friend told me she wasn't able to make it to the event due to her work schedule, but insisted that we plan a trip to visit her. I laughed and ask my friend, "so she allowing the homo in her house". My friend laughed and I could hear her in the background saying, "I know she said something smart because you laughing". She grabbed the phone from my friend and asked me what I said. I repeated the same remark to her; she laughed and said I apologized so I guess that means you will come. I told her I would and she asked if I would come by and have drinks with them the next day, so I agreed to that. The next day I joined them at my friend's house we cooked dinner, sat around, had drinks, laughed, and talked about relationships. As time passed my friend became intoxicated from the alcohol she consumed and decided to go to sleep, that left me and her bestie awake. I made the decision to go home but, my friend bestie thought it wasn't a good idea for me to leave after drinking alcohol. She took my keys and told me I was staying the night. Things felt a bit awkward because my friend was sleep and I was left up with a woman who seemed to dislike homosexuals, but I knew I had to make the best of the situation. As I started to clean the kitchen she assisted and began to ask questions about my lifestyle. I responded to them and she made it known she never engaged in the homosexual lifestyle and she had no intentions of doing it, but she went on to tell me how one of her friends in her hometown turned gay and how she didn't like being around her anymore because their friendship had changed. I asked her, "Why did the friendship change", She stated, "We don't get to do the things we use to do, because she always spending time with her girlfriend". That's when I began to tell her it wasn't her friend who changed; it was her friend lifestyle she wasn't able to accept. I told her she was homophobic and didn't have to be apart of the lifestyle because her friend was gay. I told her a prime example was me and her bestie. She told me she never looked at it that way and would straighten things out when she got home. I continued to clean the kitchen and she decided it was time for her to shower and get ready for bed, so she left me and prepared for bed. I finished cleaning, fixed another drink, and watched T.V. in the living room. When I looked up I noticed my friend's bestie coming from the bedroom with some cheerleading shorts and an aero t-shirt that was cut up to her breast and all I can see was her sexy abdomen. I was speechless; she walked in the kitchen, then came to the couch and sat in the Indian position with the grey goose bottle and two shot glasses in her hand. My eyes got big and I was a bit nervous, because I didn't know what to expect. I was thinking a woman who has no intentions being with another female would have sat on the love seat alone, so I loosened up and said, "I thought you were going to bed". She stated, "I was but the shower relaxed me so I'm going to have a few drinks." She handed me the shot glass, we took a couple of shots, and she stated "I wonder what my friend get out of being with another woman". I started to realize it was a possibility we would be fucking that night, so I responded being with a woman is magical. She replied, "How magical"? I got beside myself, all I could smell was the Victoria Secret warm and cozy hitting me in the nostrils and I kept looking at how fit her body was, I was in the mood to smash. I knew she was tipsy so I decided to respond to her question in a way that would get her mind wondering. I told her, "You'll never know how magical unless you're willing to explore the magical adventure. She looked at me and smiled and I could see in her eyes she wanted to see what the lifestyle was about. So I took a risk and grabbed the back of her head pulled her in, pushed my tongue in her mouth and French kissed her with passion behind it. She jerked back and said DAMN that was magic. I whispered, "I know you're curious, if you don't tell then I won't tell". She then responded, "What if our friend wakes up". I told her she won't she out for the night. I knew from all the nights we had went out and got drunk, there was no waking up for her. She leaned back in and we kissed with the same passion behind it, we moved from the couch to the floor. I began to nibble on her ear and behind her neck. As I gripped her body, I could tell that was her hot spot from the intense moans. I made my way down kissing her collar bone and then to her breast. Damn her breast was just like I like them, the size of grapefruits. I sucked on them until her nipples where erected and began to suck them firmly. I could tell she was loving that, because she pulled my head back leaned down and started to kiss me aggressively, and began kissing and biting on my neck while whispering my pussy is wet and I want you to fuck me. I could tell from her aggressive actions anticipation was built and she was ready to cum all over me. I was turned on by that and loved every minute of it, but I was in control so I got a bit aggressive and pushed her back, pinned her arms down and licked her lips as she reached at my tongue to kiss me. I told her I was about to eat her pussy like some ice cream and I wanted her to wet my face like that ice cream had melted. I made my way down to her pussy and licked from her U-spot up to her clit. I noticed her clit was standing at attention, every time I stroked it with my tongue her moans got louder. I continued to stroke her clit as I tongue fucked her and her body began to shake uncontrollably. She got out of control like a wild cat chasing a prey. She rolled over pushed me on my back and began to ride my tongue like she was on a raging bull. I could feel the ejaculation running from her pussy like a water fountain. I knew her pussy wanted some pressure so I flipped her over, told her to bend over in the doggy position, inserted my middle finger and began to stroke her G-spot until it was erected. Then I entered another finger which was my index finger and began to apply more pressure to her G-spot. Her G-spot swelled as I stroked it firmly and bam there it was liquids shot from her pussy like a cannon. She moaned so loud I thought she woke our friend. I knew I had come through once again, and thought my job was finish for the night until she whispered, "That's all you got". I thought man this girl is horny so I entered her with both my middle and index finger and reached all the way back on her front wall stroking her D-spot. I started gently and began to rapidly pick up speed, before I knew it her pussy had pushed out my fingers, ejaculation shot everywhere and she was flopping on the floor. I smiled because it was something pleasurable to watch and I told her that's the pleasure women get from other women. She stretched across the floor and asked me to hold her, but I told her she had to get dressed before our friend woke up. We didn't want her to know about our encounter. When she proceeded to get up her legs were so weak she fell to the floor, so I dressed her and helped her to the bathroom where she bathed and then went to sleep. After she laid in the quest bed; I kissed her on the cheek to make things that more magical, I showered and laid on the couch until the next morning. When we woke up we smiled the whole day and our friend had no idea what happened the night before. Matter of fact she don't know to this. I eventually ended up making several trips to Tupelo which ended in sexual encounters, but some kind of way we lost touch with one another. Her bestie and I friendship ended on some crazy mess, so we no longer have a friendship or speak to one another, but I still love her like a sister.

The Curious Convertor

The curious convertor is a friend I met during my college days, while I worked at Wal-Mart. This woman was sweet as pie and had a heart filled with gold. What I love most, she's outgoing, define classy, and conducted business better than any woman I've dated. It all began November, 2005, as I worked swiftly to put out freight in housewares this Monday morning, my coworker came to me with a huge smile on

her face and I asked her, "Why are you
smiling?" her smile was wide as the
Mississippi River. She was a person known
for smiling but this smile caught my
attention. That's when she began telling me
I had a secret admirer. As I continuously
asked her who, she continued to smile and
tell me she wasn't telling me. I thought I had
an idea because I knew I had a crush on one
of the department managers. Hell, I was
staying over just about everyday helping her
put away freight, knowing I was skipping
my 8:00 class. On top of that, I was doing a
lot of flirting, while she was doing a lot of
smiling. She enjoyed the conversations we
had so I knew for sure she was my secret
admirer. After telling my coworker I knew
about my secret admirer, she told me it
wasn't the department manager. I was
stunned because I didn't have my eye on
anyone else. My coworker continued to
laugh and told me my admirer comes
through every morning before she went to

her department to watch me. I was really puzzled because I had no idea someone was watching me, in fact I wondered what type of person watches someone and never speaks to them. A week had passed and eventually my coworker introduced me to my secret admirer. I could tell she was a bit shy the first time we talked, but things were quite intriguing. We talked for hours. During our conversation, I told her I was dating someone, but that didn't matter to either of us. I knew I had some whoreish ways so I jumped on the opportunity. She started calling and texting me on a regular basis, then our conversation picked up at work. She would come in early some days and I started staying late some days. One morning I received an unexpected phone call from her; she was inviting me to her house. I was thrilled about the invite, so I made a decision to see where she lived. When I arrived after given direction, I notice she had a nice home, so I knew I was going to be comfortable. After I parked in the garage, I entered into her home and sat on the couch in the living room. She followed me and sat next to me. We conversed about relationships until I felt the urge to rub between her thighs. Things got heated and her pussy became moist, we left the living room and went to the guest bedroom. I started kissing and sucking her soft lips, then I made my way to her breast until her nipples were erected. Things were sizzling, and her pussy was soaked. I pulled her by the waist to the end of the bed and licked her pussy like the butter pecan ice cream I adore. I stuck my tongue in and out of her pussy until her body became weak. Once we finish we left the bedroom and I noticed some pictures of her and a guy on the wall. I didn't inquire a bout those pictures because I thought it was family photos of her brother. I eventually left because I had to get home to my girlfriend. Our friendship grew closer over the next couple of months and it seemed we were on the verge of something good until she called me one day and things turned for the worst. When I received this phone call we talked for an half of hour and I remember telling her I love her, and she stated, "I love you too." Things got loud in the background I could hear a lot of commotion. She was arguing with a guy whom I didn't know was her husband until I overheard some of the conversation. She had got into a physical altercation with him and I felt bad about the situation, but started to feel it wasn't my problem and I was in no position to control that. Hell, she didn't inform me about a marriage. At this point I became angry and knew I was putting myself in a dangerous position, so I decided to end things with her. The next day she called me to come over, I didn't want to go because I knew I would be taking a risk but I made the decision to end things face to face. I asked her was her husband home and she told me No. I drove to her house where she was standing at the door and I began telling her, "I don't think we could be friends anymore". She cried and continuously asked me why? I got in my car and left her cold-hearted on her front steps. I did what I had to do and left without looking back. I later received phone calls from her husband who thought I was seeing his wife, but I denied it. The affair I had with this woman started to bother me because I didn't know what her husband was capable of doing. I tried to escape the situation, until one day I came home from work, and noticed my girlfriend sitting at the table with a woman. My heart rate must have dropped below normal. As I walked through the house to my bedroom, I spoke to my girlfriend and looked at my once secret lover with a strange look. I knew my world was about to end, I figured she was there to tell my girlfriend about the affair. I closed the door to my bedroom and listened closely to their conversation. I was relieved once I heard them having a friendly conversation about the Alpha Kappa Alpha sorority. My girlfriend had told me she was interested in being apart of that sorority. I guess my secret lover felt since she was apart of the sorority this was an opportunity to be close to me. For several months my lover and girlfriend developed a friendship and I made sure I stayed away from that. I finally drifted apart from my girlfriend and quit my job at Wal-Mart so that ended me having any contact with my secret lover. Six years passed, I ran into my once secret lover at a store, began talking and exchanged contact information. We started communicating again. She informed me she had divorced her husband a couple of years ago and was single. We grew closer over a couple of weeks, and then decide to date since we both were single. When we started dating I was anxious to fuck her since we didn't have many encounters when we were secret lovers. She insisted I wasn't getting any for three months. I found that quite interesting, I knew I wasn't waiting three months to get some ass. A month passed without me getting any, so I started to believe she was really putting my ass on the three month rule. One evening I invited her over, where some family and I were playing cards, when she entered she was looking astonishing. I was ready to tear her clothes off and knew at that moment the three month rule was over. I decided to end the card game and we made the decision to go back to her house. When we arrived we went straight to the bedroom. I began massaging her body until her mind escaped the three month rule. Once she felt relaxed my finger entered into her pussy and I began sucking her breast as I massage her walls. As she moaned that feel good, I moved from her breast to her pussy. I sucked her pussy as she pressed my head further in her pussy. I could tell she hadn't been sexually active in awhile. I sucked and fucked her pussy with my tongue until she squirmed. Once her body shivered, I pushed my fingers in her pussy, stoking her deep spot to give her a full body orgasm, because her body wasn't use to being stroked in that area, she did not produce. Instead I massaged these areas so her body could become familiar with that type of action. After massing her deep spot I sucked her clit until her body shivered. I wasn't pleased with the reaction I received; most of the women I dealt with were capable of producing full body and squirting orgasms. So I began to train her body on a regular until she amazed me. On this particular night it was Valentine Day. I bought wine, rose petals, candles, and prepared dinner for her. She was on her way home from work when I called her to see exactly where she was because I wasn't finished getting the house ready. I needed to run her bath water and put the rose petals in so I told her to stop at Wal-Mart and pick up some personal items. When she walked in the house she cried, then we ate dinner.

When we finished dinner we sat and drank wine, then she got in the tub where I bathed her. After her bath we drank more wine and peach Amsterdam vodka until we were intoxicated. I took her to the bedroom where I started kissing her, then down her body until I reached her feet. I would never forget sex was so passionate that night. We were making love for the first time. After kissing her feet I made my way back up to her breast and suck them until her nipples were erect. Then I massaged her body all over with oil, until she screamed fuck me. As I kissed her I inserted my middle finger and massaged her walls all over. I stroked her G-spot like I was playing a piano. She moaned and whispered fuck me as I reached her D-spot. When I realized her pussy was clamping down on my fingers I knew this was the night fireworks were going to explode. I had strapped up before she got home, so she was not aware until I pushed my dick in her pussy and started stroking her deep spot. As I thrust long and hard her pussy started clamped down on my dick and pushed my dick out as her pussy ejaculated all over my dick. She screamed damn that feel good and bent over in the doggy position. I pushed my dick in her pussy again and thrust back and forward tapping her deep spot. Before I can get in five strokes her body began to jerk as she pushed away from my dick and her body jerked uncontrollably. All I could do was smile, my love had experienced her first complete orgasm and she felt good. I immediately laid across the bed, and wrapped my arms around her while she cried and told me how much she had missed me over the years. The night went well and our lives have been great every since. We are still rocking together and hoping this is a life long commitment.

Latoya Anderson, a graduate of
Jackson State University, was raised in a
small town known as Laurel, MS. She
currently resides in Jackson, MS. A
respected role model who was inspired to
write The Untold Truth Revealed, Lifestyle
of a Lesbian to broaden the perspective of
inquiring individuals & the LGBT
community.